HEROES OF THE FORCE

THE BEST OF *STAR WARS INSIDER*
GUIDE TO THE LIGHT SIDE

TITAN
WWW.TITAN-COMICS.COM

Star Wars Insider
Heroes of the Force
ISBN: 978-1-78585-1926

Senior Executive Editor Divinia Fleary
Editor Chris Cooper
Editor at Large Jonathan Wilkins
Copy Editor Simon Hugo

Designer Russell Seal
Art Director Oz Browne
Publishing Manager Darryl Tothill
Publishing Director Chris Teather
Operations Director Leigh Baulch
Executive Director Vivian Cheung
Publisher Nick Landau

Published by Titan
A division of
Titan Publishing Group Ltd.,
144 Southwark Street,
London, SE1 0UP

Collecting material
previously published in
Star Wars Insider magazine.

A CIP catalogue record for this title is available from the British Library.

First Edition August 2017
10 9 8 7 6 5 4 3 2 1

Printed in China.

Acknowledgments
Titan would like to thank the cast and crews of the *Star Wars*
films, and the animated series: *Star Wars: The Clone Wars* and
Star Wars Rebels. A special thanks also to the teams at Dark Horse
Comics, Marvel Comics, and Del Rey for their contributions
to this book. A huge thanks also to Brett Rector, Sammy Holland, and
Michael Siglain at Lucasfilm for all of their invaluable help in putting
this volume together.

HEROES OF THE FORCE

THE BEST OF *STAR WARS INSIDER*
GUIDE TO THE LIGHT SIDE

CONTENTS

STAR WARS INSIDER

ISSUE 34 $4.50 US $5.95 CAN

Exclusive Interview!

Mark Hamill

Episode One Casting Announced!

Turn to Page 15 for a Peek at

Prequel Yoda!

MARK HAMILL
LUKE SKYWALKER

ISSUE 34
SUMMER 1997

Classic Star Wars: The Early Adventures published by Dark Horse Comics, collecting Russ Manning's newspaper strips (May)

Bantam Spectra release *Star Wars: The Paradise Snare*, the first novel in A.C. Krispin's Han Solo Trilogy (May)

Filming on *Star Wars: The Phantom Menace* begins on June 26th

No book about the Jedi could be complete without the most famous of them all: our main protagonist throughout the original *Star Wars* trilogy, Luke Skywalker.

Mark Hamill's performance as Luke over the course of those three movies is nothing short of amazing, going from whiny farm boy to dangerously sure of himself student and then calm, confident Jedi.

Hamill once complained that the end of Luke's journey was akin to the *James Bond* series finishing just as 007 is awarded his license to kill. Thankfully, after a long delay, Luke is now back in action. As Hamill says in this vintage interview, *"Star Wars* was amazing then, and it's amazing now." How true. And you can trust him. He's a Jedi.—**Jonathan Wilkins**

Mark Richard Hamill (born September 25, 1951) is an actor, writer, producer, and director. He is best known for portraying Luke Skywalker in the original Star Wars *trilogy (1977-1983), a role he reprised in* Star Wars: The Force Awakens *(2015). Hamill has forged a highly successful career as a voice actor, most notably as the Joker in the* Batman *franchise, beginning with* Batman: The Animated Series *in 1992.*

MARK HAMILL:
◆ THE
JEDI SPEAKS

"I want to come with you to Alderaan. There's nothing here for me now. I want to learn the ways of the Force and become a Jedi like my father." – Luke Skywalker (Mark Hamill), *Star Wars*

BY JACQUIE
KUBIN

ITH THOSE WORDS, AS WELL AS A ferocious determination and a powerful destiny, Mark Hamill's Luke Skywalker — the farm boy from Tatooine who becomes the hero of the Rebel Alliance — launches himself, and the first *Star Wars* trilogy, on a bold and epic adventure.

The legendary actor was only 24 when he first donned Luke's white tunic, and his boyish innocence and wide-eyed exuberance helped open the door to George Lucas' vast cinematic galaxy for a generation of young moviegoers. His are the eyes through which the audience experiences the saga (though his deep, piercing blue eyes are more expressive than most of ours), and when he learns about the mysterious yet somehow familiar "ways of the Force," so do we.

And thanks to Hamill's open and accessible acting, through which we see Luke's maturation from naïve, impatient youth to wise, masterful Jedi Knight, when he triumphs at the end of *Return of the Jedi* by defeating the Empire and helping to redeem his father, we see the limitless potential in ourselves. His victory is ours, and his heroic journey complete, when he declares, "I am a Jedi, like my father before me."

No one would dispute that point, since Hamill made the character's transformation over the course of three films remarkably believable — quite a feat when surrounded by the most ground-breaking special effects of all time. "What amazes me," Hamill told the *Insider*, "is the number of people I have met who name *Star Wars* as one of the seminal experiences that led them in their career path.

"Looking back at the first film," Hamill continued modestly, "I remember thinking then that Luke was not what we called 'an actor's role.' I didn't see it as so revolutionary, but in the context of what I had to do, I guess I did well." He did more than well. As any card-carrying member of that amorphous group reluctantly known as Generation-X will tell you,

Mark Hamill was our first real hero. (Yes, *real*.)

Today, Hamill is the hero of the young again, thanks to the *Star Wars Trilogy Special Edition*, which entranced the entire world earlier this year. Suddenly, children everywhere are thrilling for the first time at Luke's exploits on the big screen — and embracing him in much the same way their parents did 20 years ago.

"I received this wonderful outpouring of love," Hamill recalled of his arrival at the Special Edition's world premiere in Los Angeles. "It was multi-generational, from grandmothers to really young people. After seeing the movie again, I realized it's no wonder people find it so optimistic and uplifting. Far from my fear that it would appear outdated, they could have re-released the original film and people would have enjoyed it."

In fact, the star had not even seen *Star Wars* since its original theatrical release in 1977. "At first I had some trepidation about seeing it again," Hamill said from his Malibu, California, home, which he shares with Marilou, his wife of 18 years, and their kids, Nathan (17), Griffin (14), and Chelsea (8). "George and I share a trait in that we both tend to see the flaws in our work, and I was concerned over how dated it is," he continued. "Then, when I saw it on the big screen, I was astonished — I never expected to be as moved as I was. Over the years you tend to accept the mantra that it is just special effects, when, in fact, it is a really well-constructed film. Focusing on that, I saw that the film was brilliant, and I saw the great flourishes and directorial touches that George put into it."

The Jedi admitted he wasn't always in such awe of the film. "I did not recognize the importance of *Star Wars*," he said. "I did not expect the reaction that the Special Edition has received. It is not so much that I ignored *Star Wars*, but I guess

"Seeing the movie again, I saw that it's a great, warm film about friendship, family, and conquering adversity.'

I was just concentrating on other things, on continuing my career as an actor, not necessarily as Luke Skywalker." Then something clicked. "I was watching a special with [original Mickey Mouse Club member] Annette Funnicello," he continued, "and I thought, 'Once a Mousketeer, always a Mousketeer' — even though her role as a Mousketeer was short in comparison with her entire career as an actress and singer. She is comfortable with that, as I am now comfortable with my work in *Star Wars*."

It wasn't always that way. For years, Hamill shied away from his *Star Wars* legacy, fearful of falling into Hollywood's type-casting trap. Eager to define himself as a diverse, multi-dimensional actor, he went to Broadway, playing Mozart in *Amadeus* and John Merrick in *The Elephant Man*, and eventually to the world of voice-over acting, where he made his strongest mark as the Joker in Warner Brothers' acclaimed hit, *Batman: The Animated Series* and its spin-off feature film, *Mask of the Phantasm*. He also created the Dark Horse comic *Black Pearl*, which he is planning to turn into a feature film he will direct.

But Hamill said he soon realized that, while he certainly didn't want to rest on his laurels, an association with *Star Wars* was nothing to hide. "I don't know why I tended to run from it for so long," the actor reflected. "Seeing the movie again, I saw that it's a great, warm film about friendship, family, and conquering adversity. I look at the trilogy and the character with great fondness today. I know that *Star Wars* was amazing then and it's amazing now."

Still, even during the time of the first *Star Wars* trilogy's initial release, Hamill filled his off years with projects a galaxy away from the saga — and admirably resisted the temptation to cash in by starring in any number of the third-rate, *Star Wars* rip-off projects he was offered. In 1978, he starred in the raucous Las Vegas teen adventure-comedy *Corvette Summer*, which found Hamill hooking up with a sassy hooker (*Ghostbusters'* Annie Potts) on the hunt for his custom-built Stingray after the 'vette is stolen by car thieves. The film was a can't-miss proposition for Hamill's then-young fans, who salivated at the idea of Luke Skywalker in a car movie.

Hamill also starred with Lee Marvin and Robert Carradine in the revered director Samuel Fuller's World War II tale *The Big Red One* (1980), and with fellow 1970s icon Kristy McNichol (*Family, Little Darlings*) in the 1981 barroom brawler *The Night the Lights Went Out in Georgia*.

Between his film work and appearances on Broadway (he did *The Elephant Man* in 1981 and *Amadeus* in 1983), the actor managed to squeeze in a few more *Star Wars*-related projects. In addition to appearing in the notorious "*Star Wars* Holiday Special" in 1978 and hosting the CBS documentary *SPFX: The Empire Strikes Back* in 1980, Hamill reprised Luke Skywalker in National Public Radio's acclaimed 13-episode adaptation of *Star Wars* in 1981 — one of the most successful NPR dramas ever aired. He also participated in NPR's *Empire* adaptation, which aired in early 1983.

Though Hamill is proud of his work on the *Star Wars* radio dramas, nothing could compare with his experiences making the actual films, he said. "The relationship between Carrie and Harrison and myself was so wonderful," said the actor who is well-known throughout the entertainment

"On Broadway, I was able to play the Elephant Man, Mozart, the Groucho Marx role from *Room Service*."

industry as one of the nicest guys in Hollywood. Looking back at the *Star Wars* shoot in 1976, Hamill recalled the film's initial production, in which Hamill acted primarily with Anthony Daniels and Alec Guinness before joining up with the rest of the cast in London.

"I remember with particular fondness," he said, "working with Anthony Daniels in the desert. We were there with the rest of the crew, yet pretty much on our own, and I would say that we bonded there. We were the younger people on the movie, and I think sometimes [in England] we would feel left out. But we had our times together in the desert, and seeing the movie again I realized how much I enjoyed working with him then and how much I miss the guy now."

Daniels concurred. "Mark and I used to drive to work together in the desert," Daniels recalled, "and we would laugh about each other's lines, because they seemed so corny. Working on the film, we did scenes in bits and pieces that were chronologically out of order, so sometimes it seemed that the whole thing was rather silly. Of course," Daniels quipped, "I would get the last laugh, because I could actually say my lines without any one seeing me wince under the costume."

If Hamill was wincing at a scenario that found him sharing most of screen time with two odd-couple droids, he didn't show it onscreen. Indeed, the believability of Luke's relationship with C-3PO and R2-D2 was crucial in allowing the audience to accept much of what was presented in *Star Wars*. Said Daniels, "One of the reasons that C-3PO worked so well was that Mark treated C-3PO as a real person. Throughout the movies, we often see Threepio through Luke's eyes, and his treatment of the character went along way toward giving

Threepio a humanity."

After completing the first *Star Wars* trilogy, Hamill, feeling pigeonholed as a heroic leading man, returned almost immediately to Broadway, even singing and dancing in the 1985 musical *Harrigan & Hart*, which earned him a Drama Desk nomination. "I went to Broadway because that's where I found the comedic roles that I wanted to do," Hamill said. "I wasn't getting the really interesting character roles that I wanted in film. But on Broadway, I was able to play the Elephant Man, Mozart, the Groucho Marx role from *Room Service*. They were all challenging for me, which is what I wanted as an actor."

Despite the glamor of the stage, Hamill found even more challenges behind the microphone, as a voice-over artist. In fact, his career as a voice-over actor had begun before *Star Wars*, with the 1973-75 CBS cartoon *Jeannie*, Hanna-Barbera's spin-off of *I Dream of Jeannie*, in which Hamill provided the voice of Corry, who discovers a magic genie and her huge but bumbling apprentice Babu. But it was *Batman: The Animated Series*, the 1992 Fox Network cartoon in which Hamill's howling, cackling portrayal of the Joker almost stole the show from the Dark Knight himself, that firmly established Hamill as one of the top voice-over talents in the industry.

"Voice-over work is not unlike the original radio dramas," Hamill said, "and I consider it to be acting at its purest. My generation of actors missed out on radio acting to a large extent, and I am glad to be doing this type of work now. It's extremely challenging, because the emotion and the humanity of the character is expressed only using the voice. You can't rely on physical actions to portray the character."

Hamill, who also voiced the Joker in both the *Batman* animated feature film and Sega Genesis game, recently reprised the role in an episode of the WB network's new *Superman* cartoon in which

"Voice-over work is not unlike the original radio dramas, and I consider it to be acting at its purest."

Batman and Superman join forces. "It's interesting how the writers were able to team up these two men, one being a super-power and the other a mortal," he said. "There is a real dichotomy they created when they have Bruce Wayne and Lois Lane have a fling. Joker, in this cartoon, is extremely flamboyant and over-the-top."

The actor also revealed that there's plenty more Joker on the way. "There is going to be a new batch of animated *Batman* cartoons released, following the last two-year lull," Hamill said. "I think the produc-

ers wanted to hold back on creating new episodes until the Fox contract ran out, so they could take the show to the WB network. I recently did my first Joker in two years, and it was fun."

After taking on the Joker, Hamill's voice-over career really took flight. He plays Col. Christopher Blair in Origin System's blockbuster CD-ROM adventure games *Wing Commander III: Heart of the Tiger* and *Wing Commander IV: The*

Price of Freedom. The success of the games led to Hamill reprising the role in the USA network's 13-episode animated series *Wing Commander: Academy*. "When I first began work on Wing Commander, I knew it would be a hit," he confided. "But its success surprised even me." He recently completed his final installment: *Wing Commander: Prophecy*.

Continuing his forays into the digital realm, Hamill can also be heard on the Sci-Fi Channel's web site, Dominion (*www.scifi.com*), narrating a multimedia version of Franz Kafka's "The Country Doctor" on the site's Seeing Ear Theater. "Mark really works within all the different media that are of interest to many computer users," said Sci-Fi Channel's Sharon Levy.

But surprisingly, Hamill sees his work on Bruce Willis' 1996 cartoon *Bruno the Kid*, as one of his greatest achievements in animation. "*Bruno the Kid* was a milestone in my career," he said, "because I was utilized to do three different voices, which means that I am capable of being what is called a 'utility player' — an actor who can do voices, accents, and provide versatility on command. It's taken me four years of hard work to get to that level."

But the actor concedes, "You have to be careful what you wish for. Now, three to four days a week, I'm doing voice-overs. Right now, I'm busy working on the animated *Blues Brothers* for UPN." The prime-time series follows the adventures of John Belushi and Dan Aykroyd's classic characters, who originated on NBC's *Saturday Night Live* before embarking on a concert tour, a string of successful albums, and their own classic 1980 feature film (called, appropriately, *The Blues Brothers*).

The cartoon *Blues Brothers* recasts Aykroyd & the late Belushi with their brothers, Peter and Jim, and also features the voice talents of original *SNL* stars Laraine Newman and Don Novello. But it's Hamill who is providing many of the series

"When I first began work on Wing Commander, I knew it would be a hit."

'utility' voices — and earning the praise of his co-stars. "Talking with Mark and hearing the quality of his voice and the rate of his speech during regular conversation, you would never know this guy is one of the most versatile voice-over talents in Los Angeles," enthused Jim Belushi. "He can do probably 50 characters — change his voice rate, quality, tone. His throat is like six different instruments in an orchestra. He has an amazing instrument — and he's funny."

Proving that point, Hamill recently appeared on *Saturday Night Live*, playing himself (to wild audience applause) in a home-shopping spoof in which *SNL* cast members Will Ferrell and Chris Kattan attempt to auction off a "real Mark Hamill" to *Star Wars* memorabilia collectors. He also put in a hilarious cameo on CBS' *Late Show with David Letterman*, again playing himself in a fictitious new series that featured Hamill directing parallel parking on a busy city street, and on NBC's hit alien sitcom *3rd Rock from the Sun*.

But while the Special Edition has put Hamill in more demand than ever, the star is staying focused on his graphic novel *Black Pearl*, which he originally penned as a screenplay. His desire to take over the role of director on a *Black Pearl* feature stems from his Broadway experience in *Harrigan & Hart* — and from the wisdom of his children. "*Harrigan & Hart* changed my attitude about not being able to have a say-so in the production," he said. "I was in dual productions of the show, and when we moved to Broadway, I really felt that some of the changes they made were wrong. But I was only a player and did not have the authority to say anything about it." Instead, like Luke witnessing the death of his friend Biggs, Hamill had no choice but to watch the show go down in flames.

"In deciding that I wanted to direct *The Black Pearl*," he

explained, "I accepted the fact that if I do not own something, then I do not have the right to dictate what is right and wrong. One evening, while driving home from a movie, I was discussing the film with my children — actually, I was pointing out all the flaws that I saw. As only children can, they said, "Dad, if you think you could do better, why don't you just do it?' So I am going to give it a try on this project.

"My original concept," Hamill continued, "was to film it in L.A. with a hand-held camera — a lean, mean modest budget film that would be independent and could break the rules of the major studios. I wanted to keep the budget modest and concentrate on the story while making a comment on personal responsibility and the nation's appetite for one tawdry, sleazy story that exploits the worst in man, versus seeking the story about what is the best in man. Our fascination with the lurid subject matters of talk and tabloid shows is another wrinkle in our national fabric."

Though he's built up a sterling reputation behind the scenes, Hamill has not completely shied away from the camera. He has starred in several independent films, including *The Guyver* and *Midnight Ride*, and of course he was the star of 1997's first $100+ million blockbuster, the *Star Wars* Special Edition, which recently had its gala, Royal premiere in London. Hamill attended, along with Lucas, Daniels, Peter Mayhew (Chewie), Kenny Baker (Artoo) — and Britain's Prince Charles.

"It was interesting to sit next to Prince Charles, who commented all throughout the movie," Hamill said of the U.K. premiere. "In one scene, where we were all running to the *Millennium Falcon* for a fast getaway, he remarked 'I sure could use a plane that takes off that fast.' He seemed amused by the film. He doesn't really laugh out loud, but he makes these more dignified chuckles of satisfaction. Because of the way he kept commenting to me, I felt so relaxed with him, and I let my guard down and started making comments back — which I was told would be against protocol. At one point, I said to him, 'Gee, I am really sorry your boys could not come.'"

Yet as exciting as that event was, it's the Special Edition's world premiere in Los Angeles that Hamill remembers best, probably because he got to bring his entire family. His children's response to the premiere not only pleased, but also

Left: Will Ferrell, Mark Hamill, and Chris Kattan spoof home shopping on Saturday Night Live.

Right top: Hamill as Col. Christopher Blair in the popular Wing Commander CD-ROM series.

Right bottom: A cover from Hamill's Black Pearl comic series from Dark Horse Comics.

"Right now I am living moment-to-moment and waiting to see what comes up next."

Top: Hamill and wife Marilou at the *Star Wars Special Edition* Royal Premiere in London. Bottom: At home in Malibu, CA with Marilou and daughter Chelsea.

surprised him. "My children were excited about going to the premiere with me, which I found great," Hamill enthused. "What really surprised me was Nathan, my oldest son. He's at that 'cool' age where he has a girlfriend and he's in a band. But just before the premiere, he stunned me when he asked if he could go into the attic and get my Luke Skywalker boots to wear to the premiere. Griffin, my second, was at first nonchalant, originally saying that he was not going to the premiere because it was at 10:30 AM on a Saturday morning and he planned to sleep in." Eventually, all attended the event quite happily. "My youngest, Chelsea, really enjoyed the film," he added proudly.

Nathan was just three years old at the end of the filming of *Return of the Jedi*. "I wonder, looking back on the photographs, what he remembers," Nathan's dad said. "Even though he was very young, he did go through the on-set experience and he has been a fan of the movies as he was growing up. I guess I was taken aback when he became so excited again with the re-release of the movies. I think he might wish he had been a little bit older so that he could remember more about that time."

But in keeping with his resolve to look forward, Mark Hamill does not often peer back. "I am not the kind of person who goes through scrapbooks or yearbooks," he said, "and I think my kids know that it is not one of my favorite things to do. Although last year, Chelsea came running into my room and said, 'Dad, quick! You're on TV when you were a little boy! She was watching reruns of *The Partridge Family*, and I was appearing as one of the girls' date. I was about 18 at the time."

But while vintage versions of the actor are delighting audiences the world over, Hamill is keeping his focus on the printed page. "I have a lot of writing projects that I have started," he revealed. "Now that the re-write of *Black Pearl* is finished and at the point where it's in other peoples' hands, I'm turning toward other projects. I have developed an animated television series, and I even have a game that I have written up. Right now, I am living moment-to-moment and waiting to see what comes up next."

Star Wars fans seem to be doing the same thing — much to Hamill's chagrin. The actor says he is commonly asked the same question by people he meets: "When is the next one?" Said Hamill, "That is thanks to George numbering the first film Episode Four. If the movies would have kept coming out every three years, as originally planned, we would be finishing up the series by now, as there were originally nine stories in all. I remember telling people back in 1977 that we are in the middle trilogy of three trilogies, and that the characters in the 'book-end' trilogies would not be the same as in films four, five and six.

"But no matter how many times you say that," he continued, "people still say to you 'Why isn't the Princess going to be in the next one? Why isn't Luke?' No matter how many times I have said it, you are always going to meet people who don't know and want it to be the continuing adventures of Luke, Han, Princess Leia, Lando, Chewbacca, R2-D2 and C-3PO."

That's no surprise, since even 20 years later, audiences are still captivated by the *Star Wars* saga and by Hamill's wide-eyed performance. Mark Hamill knows that no matter how accomplished he is as an actor, writer, director, producer, or voice-over artist, there will always be legions of fans who know him and love him as Luke Skywalker.

And — so long as those take the time to check out what he's doing now — that's perfectly fine with him. Clearly, in all of Hamill's endeavors, the Force has been with him. Always. ✦

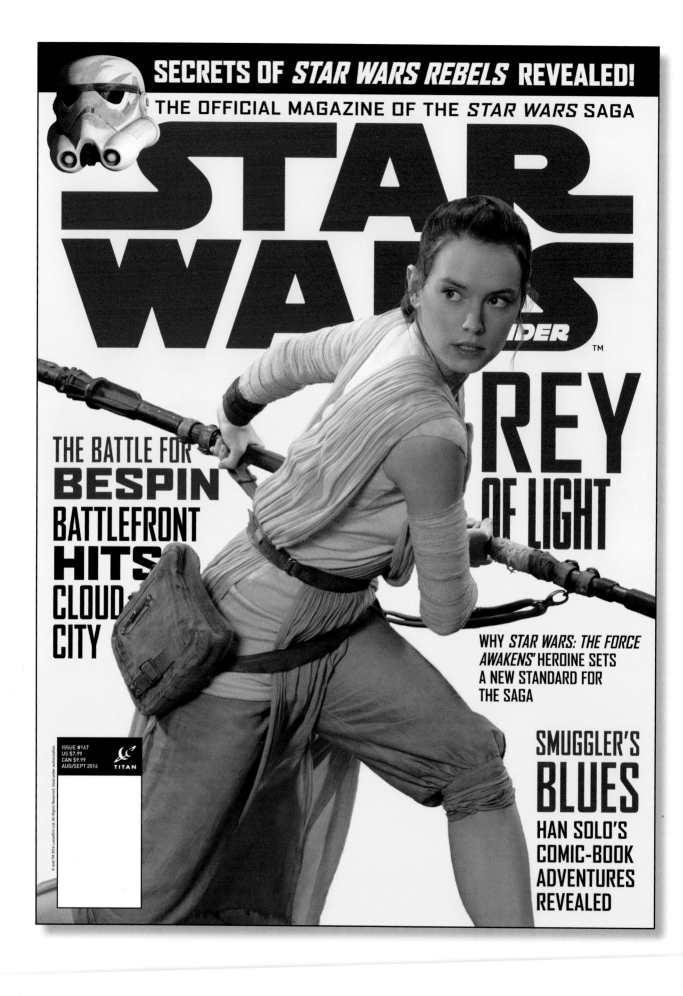

THE OFFICIAL MAGAZINE OF THE *STAR WARS* SAGA

STAR WARS

INSIDER™

REY OF LIGHT

THE BATTLE FOR BESPIN
BATTLEFRONT HITS CLOUD CITY

WHY *STAR WARS: THE FORCE AWAKENS'* HEROINE SETS A NEW STANDARD FOR THE SAGA

SMUGGLER'S BLUES
HAN SOLO'S COMIC-BOOK ADVENTURES REVEALED

ISSUE #167
US $7.99
CAN $9.99
AUG/SEPT 2016

Titan

REY
A HERO'S JOURNEY (SO FAR)

ISSUE 167/168
AUG/SEP 2016

The Chewbacca Story, a young readers book by Benjamin Harper published (August)

Original R2-D2 actor Kenny Baker passed away on August 13th

September 30th sees the second Force Friday event, celebrating the forthcoming release of *Rogue One: A Star Wars Story*

Star Wars Art: Ralph McQuarrie published by Abrams Books, with a foreword by George Lucas (September)

An enigma wrapped in a mystery, we'd all like to know just who Rey is and what part she will play in galactic events. But that's all still to come—and isn't not knowing and wildly speculating kind of the best part?

We'll learn more about Rey in *Star Wars: The Last Jedi*, but so far we only have *The Force Awakens* to go by, and in the following exploration all-round *Star Wars* expert Tricia Barr peels back the layers to reveal what a groundbreaking and fascinating character Rey already is. No doubt there will be plenty of room for future examinations of Rey's character as the films offer further revelations. I wonder what sort of article Tricia will write then?

—Jonathan Wilkins

Daisy Jazz Isobel Ridley (born April 10, 1992) has appeared as "Fran Bedingfield" in the BBC series, Casualty, *"Roxy Starlet" in* Mr Selfridge *and in* Lifesaver, *which was nominated for a BAFTA Award, and music videos before being cast as Rey in the* Star Wars *sequel trilogy.*

BEFORE A HERO CAN
TAKE A SINGLE STEP,
THEY MUST BE CRAFTED
WITH THE POTENTIAL
TO WITHSTAND THE TESTS
TO FOLLOW. IN HER
ONGOING SERIES ON THE
HERO'S JOURNEY, TRICIA
BARR EXAMINES THE
FOUNDATION OF *THE FORCE
AWAKENS'* BREAKOUT
CHARACTER, REY.

FOOTPRINTS IN THE SAND: IMPRESSIONS OF REY

I magine Rey's life story as footprints across the Jakku desert. Over time, the elements have erased or blurred her earliest tracks and left behind only what we see in *The Force Awakens*. What comes after this brief glimpse lies beyond the rise of a dune—to be discovered at a later time. Over the years, this occasional series of articles has evaluated the long, winding paths of many characters. But as Rey, Finn, Poe Dameron, and Kylo Ren begin brand new adventures in a brand new trilogy, we are granted a fresh

opportunity to explore a monomyth from its very beginnings. Rather than following in the footsteps of these characters, we can walk beside them on their journey.

As we navigate the shifting sands, character development will be our focus. This begins with the drawing-board stage, where a storyteller determines who each character is and what motivates them. These motivations do not need to be spelled out for the audience at the beginning of a tale, but they must become apparent along the way. Motivations can change significantly during an adventure, and pivotal moments must be carefully deployed. While sudden shifts in a character's heroic journey should be surprising, they must also be born out of the

fundamental traits established by more gradual development. No single trait is enough to make a character interesting, but in combination they can create compelling heroes such as Rey.

SHOW AND TELL

When introducing a character, the storyteller has two devices at his or her disposal: showing the audience events that reveal information about the character and telling them pertinent facts. The latter is best used sparingly, and informs the well-known storyteller's maxim: "Show, don't tell."

Early on in *The Force Awakens* we see Rey dragging her scavenged loot to and from her speeder. This shows

she has a job—or at least a purpose—and that she is physically strong. Later, when she and Finn are fleeing Niima Outpost, he says, "We need a pilot," and Rey tells him—and us—"We've got one." This brief telling of information leads into an extended sequence of showing, with Rey running up the *Millennium Falcon*'s ramp, ordering Finn to the gunner station, and her hopping into the pilot's seat and quickly taking the freighter aloft.

Examples of similar tells followed by shows from *A New Hope* include Han telling Obi-Wan about the *Falcon*'s speed capabilities before escaping Imperial pursuit on Tatooine, and Luke telling Wedge he used to bulls-eye womp rats in his T-16 before making the impossible shot that destroys the first Death Star.

By the time Rey guides the *Falcon* in its hair-raising escape from Niima Outpost, the story has already laid the groundwork to prepare the audience for the thrilling chase through the ship graveyard. Rey first appears with her face obscured by a mask, in a shot tightly framed behind a hatch she is opening. This first impression doesn't definitively imply gender, but the costume suggests practicality and a little flair (see sidebar). Rey clings to a nearly vertical wall, then jumps across to a rope. As the camera angle shifts, it reveals that she is descending into a massive man-made cavern. This person is shown to be brave, maybe even reckless. Immediately we know that—whoever this is—they share some of the attributes we associate with being a pilot of the *Millennium Falcon*.

When she is back outside, Rey unmasks and bangs the last drops of water from her canteen. She may be brave, but she is still vulnerable to the elements. A wide shot reveals her location as a ruined Star Destroyer in an otherwise featureless desert. She is isolated—not only geographically but also from the heart of the action. The ship is a relic and the battle that downed it is long over. This sense is reinforced as Rey dines alone in the shell of an AT-AT. It is a stark contrast to *The Phantom Menace* and *A New Hope*, where food is used to bring family dynamics into focus. Image after image frames our hero as small, from her speeder passing the starship graveyard to her standing below Unkar Plutt waiting for her trade. Combined with a lack of dialogue during Rey's first minutes on screen, the imagery leaves us in no doubt about the harsh, empty world that Rey inhabits.

Yet, while contrasts such as Rey's lonely meal reinforce the idea that we are seeing something new, images such as Rey on her speeder hark back to previous films in the *Star Wars* saga. It is not uncommon for movies to draw on well-known archetypes to create a visual lexicon to which the audience can relate, but *Star Wars* is in the unique position of being able to draw from its own widely recognized iconography. Previously, both Luke and Anakin had guided their own speeders across desert landscapes (dressed in similar attire) before setting out on adventures that put their piloting skills to more dramatic use.

By the time Rey points the *Falcon* toward space, our time spent with her on Jakku has established many of the traits that will drive her character arc in the future. The vulnerability on Rey's face as she scrubs her scavenged wares reappears in Maz's castle on Takodana. Her self-sufficiency comes back into play following her escape from Kylo Ren's torture chamber on Starkiller Base. Most importantly, the self-belief that has sustained her during perilous scavenger hunts on Jakku continues to serve her well when she summons the courage to close her eyes and call upon the Force to help her defeat Kylo Ren.

A DIFFERENT TYPE OF HERO

As so far revealed in *The Force Awakens*, Rey shares many characteristics with her predecessor protagonists, Anakin and Luke. However, she exists in a wider world of storytelling (across all media) where female characters do not share parity with their male counterparts in either quantity or quality. In the past few years, the White House and the United Nations have championed initiatives to promote STEM (science, technology, engineering

Taking aim! Rey takes on the First Order during a pivotal scene in *The Force Awakens*.

THE SCAVENGER
COSTUME

Movie costumes aren't just clothes: they are visual clues about the character wearing them. Even before they knew Rey's name, fans had already been inspired to make their own version of the costume based on brief glimpses of the character from the very first teaser trailer. Before the movie opened in theaters, *Insider* asked a couple of cosplayers what the scavenger attire told them about Rey as a character.

Lisa Curtis Saunders: It's certainly given me an appreciation for her resourcefulness, learning all the details of the costume and the purposes behind them. It's a comfortable, practical costume for a tough, practical lady. Beyond that it's hard to know, but I am ridiculously excited to find out.

Kay Serna: With some of the complications figuring out how all the elements fit together, I had to believe everything she wore was for a reason beyond just looking good on film. As I found all the pieces I needed for my costume build, I felt connected to Rey—being resourceful, making things work. When I put on the whole ensemble, I knew that much more about what it's like to be her: how the fabrics make you stand; the range of movement she has. I even learned the hard way where she needs to wear the equivalent of sunscreen! From *Star Wars* color theory, I knew Rey is a hero. Just from the costume you can tell she's practical, clever, and not afraid of getting dirty.

Taking on Kylo Ren
in the thrilling final
confrontation.

and math) careers for women. In storytelling, particularly on television, the number of female characters shown to have STEM specialisms is increasing. But often these roles are defined in relation to a male protagonist's story arc, for example Felicity Smoak in *Arrow* or Amy Farrah Fowler in *The Big Bang Theory*. In the original trilogy, Leia participates in repairs on the *Falcon* but she isn't intended to be a mechanically gifted character like Rey—who fixes a dangerous leak and prevents the hyperdrive from blowing. Rey is a STEM protagonist in the same way as Anakin in the prequel trilogy, but because she is front and center as a STEM female, she offers a more progressive role model for male and female viewers alike.

Throughout *The Force Awakens*, Rey resists bullies: from Unkar Plutt and his thugs who want to take BB-8 to Kylo Ren who wishes to take things from her mind against her will. Her own experience gives her empathy with others who are struggling against powerful forces—not only BB-8 and Finn, but also the largely absent Luke to whom she is inexorably drawn. Of course, such characters are not unique to *Star Wars*; but this is by no means the only heroic archetype, and for Rey to be molded along those lines shows a clear dramatic intent. It is surely no coincidence that during production of *The Force Awakens* two of the guests who visited the set were Katie Goldman—the young girl whose schoolmates told her that *Star Wars* was "just for boys"— and Malala Yousafzai—the Nobel Prize-winning activist for female education who grew up under repressive Taliban rule in Pakistan.

"CLASSIFIED, REALLY? ME TOO."

One of the most exciting things about our journey with Rey is that it is only just beginning. Though we think we have a clear idea of the major players by the end of *The Force Awakens*, we also know that *Star Wars* has a track record of defying our initial expectations. We believed that Padmé was a handmaiden and had no reason to doubt the story that Obi-Wan told about the fate of Luke's father. We could not have imagined that Leia would be revealed as Luke's sister, either. But clues are often hidden in plain sight, and when it comes to Rey there are moments when she is clearly less forthcoming than she might be. After she saves Finn from the rathtar, she brushes off the blast door closing as lucky. Later, when Finn asks how she got away from Kylo Ren on Starkiller Base, she answers: "I can't explain it. And you wouldn't believe it." Just like Finn, the audience doesn't know everything about Rey, and probably won't for a few more years. In other words, "This is where the fun begins!"

A HEROINE'S JOURNEY

REY'S ADVENTURE BEGINS

USING THE OPENING ACT OF REY'S ADVENTURE IN *THE FORCE AWAKENS*, TRICIA BARR CONTINUES HER EXPLORATION OF THE HERO'S JOURNEY.

In a January 2013 tweet, Slashfilm's Peter Sciretta posed a question: "Who said the lead character in *Star Wars:* Episode VII is going to be a male star?" The internet reacted. In some circles very enthusiastically, in other places not so favorably. Speaking shortly after the opening of *The Force Awakens*, screenwriter Michael Arndt confirmed that the earliest story pitch from Kathleen Kennedy had been an "origin story of a female Jedi."

Storytelling is an organic process, which often involves running toward an idea you love only to watch it blow up magnificently or fizzle into an ignominious nothingness. Arndt has also noted that his earliest versions of the script involved Luke joining Rey's journey earlier in the movie, but that "any time Luke showed up, it suddenly became his movie." And that was not the story he, Lawrence Kasdan, and J.J. Abrams wanted to tell. Kasdan himself said, in a 2015 interview with *Vanity Fair*, that screenwriting requires a willingness to "kill your darlings"—and if Abrams' 'darling' was a story featuring Luke Skywalker, then the creative discovery that brought Rey's journey into focus was that Luke was not a companion on that journey, but the device or "MacGuffin" that drove it.

THE ART OF STORYTELLING

Though art constantly aspires to break the mold, there are fundamental guiding principles that help make artworks in any format understandable and relatable.

In *Return of the Jedi*, C-3PO sits before the Ewoks, gesturing with his golden hands as R2-D2 produces various sound effects. The scene represents the ways in which the earliest stories were told, and—though we don't speak Ewok—the droid's visuals and sounds form a story that the audience recognizes because we have seen it before.

That is how storytelling works best: threading together familiar elements to form a new experience that moves us emotionally. This is why no words are needed in the early part of *The Force Awakens*, where Rey moves about in her AT-AT home. A young woman eating alone, countless etchings on the wall to mark the passage of time, a free moment spent leaning against the foot of a weapon of war: These brief glimpses all suggest a very particular life, not heroic, but completely human, inspiring empathy and understanding in the audience.

The earliest storytellers were limited by the amount of time the audience was willing to invest in listening, and perhaps their own ability to keep talking. The earliest writers were limited by resources: immobile cave walls and stone tablets, then portable papyrus, which had to be manufactured by hand. The dawn of the printing press saw the first stirrings of mass production, leading to the explosion of the mass media in the 20th century. Mythologist Joseph Campbell studied storytelling across this vast history and distilled the framework of myths down to common thematic beats in his 1949 book, *The Hero With A Thousand Faces*.

George Lucas made explicit reference to Campbell's "monomyth" structure when conceiving *Star Wars*, and established that the concept could be applied to moviemaking in the same way as it applied to oral storytelling and prose. Given the

success of *Star Wars*, it didn't take long for other filmmakers to latch onto its potential, and in 1985, studio storytelling consultant Christopher Vogler set out a Hollywood moviemaking formula in a memo entitled "A Practical Guide to Joseph Campbell's *The Hero With a Thousand Faces*."

Today the internet is home to a dizzying array of articles on the Hero's Journey, but few do a better job of explaining the elements of mythic structure and how they fit together than Vogler. He expanded his memo into a bestselling book (see sidebar), and—in both works—he doesn't simply analyze the nature of stories; he explains the mechanics of making them.

ALWAYS IN MOTION, THE FUTURE IS

It's possible to envision Vogler as the Maz Kanata to a *Star Wars* fandom weaned on Campbell's monomyth. But as Maz tells Rey to look ahead for the belonging she seeks, Vogler reminds us to look behind. Throughout history, storytelling has served as a tool to help model society and to inculcate ways of behavior. Stories have been used to keep people in line, to reinforce notions that only some people are destined for greatness, and to warn against rocking the boat. For every story that serves as a rallying cry or a trigger for social change, there is another that perpetuates the status quo—even if it does so unintentionally. In 1977, *Star Wars* reminded moviegoers that individuals could rise up against oppression—and that their number could include farm boys, down-at-heel hustlers, and independent women. However, in the latter category it helped if you were a princess, and if you were looking for wider social representation... Well, it helped if you were a Wookiee or a droid. The civil rights campaign of the 1950s and the subsequent feminist movement had destroyed their fair share of Death Stars, but the struggle to right wrongs —or simply to change people's perspectives—was only just beginning.

As an advocate for better representations of women in science-fiction and fantasy stories, I have sometimes felt like Finn in *The Force Awakens*, bemoaning everyone's desire to go back to Jakku.

As recently as five years ago, well-crafted heroic journeys for female characters were harder to come by than full portions at Niima Outpost. It didn't help that Campbell's model framed women as distractions from greatness ("Woman as Temptress") or unrealistic and unhealthy expressions of love ("Meeting with the Goddess"). Vogler's original memo template doesn't address gender specifically, but over the years his revised books highlight journeys for heroes and heroines alike. The third edition of *The Writer's Journey* identifies feminist scholars and their writings on the Hero's Journey, and employs a simple yet effective technique of splitting his explanations of the journey between male and female pronouns.

"I'M NO ONE."

The early grumblings from some quarters about the prospect of a female-led trilogy of *Star Wars* movies proved to be isolated and unrepresentative, and Rey and her heroism have been embraced by the public at large, including longstanding *Star Wars* fans and new ones. Yet, for fans to hoot and cheer when the lightsaber slaps into her hand in the movie's third act, the character needed to grab the audience's heart in the first act. *The Force Awakens* does this by mostly conforming to Vogler and Campbell's structures. Vogler's Act One includes segments called "Ordinary World," "Call to Adventure," "Refusal of the Call," "Meeting with the Mentor," and "Crossing the Threshold." Campbell calls this initial phase of the journey "The Departure," and includes an extra segment: "Belly of the Whale."

Those sparse opening sequences with Rey on Jakku establish her "Ordinary World," prior to her "Call to Adventure," as she leans against the AT-AT's foot and hears the cries of BB-8, rushing across the dunes

THE EVOLUTION OF THE HERO'S JOURNEY

For many fans of *Star Wars*, their familiarity with the Hero's Journey comes from the Skywalker saga. When writing the tale that became *A New Hope*, George Lucas drew upon the work of Joseph Campbell, and this influence became widely known thanks to *The Power of Myth*, a 1988 Bill Moyers PBS miniseries and book, and the Smithsonian traveling exhibit, *Star Wars: The Magic of Myth*, during the decade that followed.

Campbell studied myths and legends from all around the world to generate what he called the "monomyth." Examining the paths of many protagonists from humble origins to epic destiny, Campbell broke down the stages of the Hero's Journey based on patterns and themes that he observed to be common across many cultures and millennia of storytelling. When Lucas sought to create his modern myth, *Star Wars*, he found much that resonated in Campbell's writing.

Due in no small part to the groundbreaking success of *Star Wars*, movies have become the largest canvas upon which

contemporary storytellers can depict their epic tales. It is no surprise, therefore, that the Hero's Journey has adapted to today's foremost mythic medium.

A graduate of the same University of Southern California film school as George Lucas, Christopher Vogler became a screenwriter, story consultant, and Hollywood development executive. In 1985 he wrote an internal memo for Disney studio execs explaining how Campbell's framework could serve as the template for successful movies of all kinds. The memo's influence quickly took off well beyond Disney's gates, and its most recent form is the third edition of Vogler's lengthy book, *The Writer's Journey: Mythic Structure for Writers*. Approaching the Hero's Journey from the perspective of modern storytelling in movies, Vogler focuses its stages around the three-act structure of films and illustrates with examples as wide-ranging as *The Wizard of Oz*, *Titanic*, *Beverly Hills Cop*, *The Lion King*—and, of course, *A New Hope* and the rest of the *Star Wars* saga.

to save him. Her "Refusal of the Call" comes as she rebuffs BB-8's attempts to team up with her. Vogler describes the "Refusal of the Call" as being based in fear, and Rey's fear is of making personal connections —as seen again later when she rips her hand away from Finn's.

The next step, "Meeting with the Mentor," was originally named by Campbell as "Supernatural Aid." Vogler's update reflects the fact that modern mythmaking doesn't necessarily need divine intervention or supernatural beings. (Marvel's *The Avengers*, for example, inverts the trope by having mortal Nick Fury mentor demigod Thor.)

In *The Force Awakens*, Rey's mentor is Han Solo. Before she meets him, though, she experiences Campbell's "Belly of the Whale," a literal swallowing into the unknown as the ship she has stolen, the *Millennium Falcon*, disappears inside a massive space freighter. In *A New Hope*, Luke has already teamed up with his mentor, Obi-Wan Kenobi, when he enters the bowels of the Death Star. The lesson here is that, for all its seeming rigidity, the Hero's Journey remains fluid, and the monomyth structure merely a guide. Rey meets Han inside the Belly of the Whale, where her mentor imparts his knowledge—in this case his non-Jedi's understanding of the supernatural forces at work in the galaxy. Mentors often pass along a talisman to use on the heroic quest, and for Luke this was his father's lightsaber. For Rey, it could be seen as the blaster Han gives her on Takodana, or it could be the *Millennium Falcon* itself, passed on in stages throughout the story.

The final stage of Vogler's first act, "The Crossing of the Threshold," occurs with the help of the mentor. This is the point where Rey fully commits to the adventure that was offered when she responded to BB-8's initial cries for help. Like Luke agreeing to accompany Obi-Wan to Alderaan, Rey steps past her reluctance to leave behind her ordinary life (even when she initially agrees to go with BB-8, she insists that it will only be a brief distraction from her daily cares) and accepts the path of the unknown.

It is at this stage that Vogler's take on the Hero's Journey and Campbell's original begin to diverge significantly. After the first act, Rey's path takes her to Takodana, where she encounters archetypal "Tests," "Enemies," "Allies," and a character-defining "Ordeal." Campbell's model focuses on both the transformation this brings and the reintegration back into the ordinary world that follows. However, Vogler dispenses with the reintegration and makes his version all about the excitement of the silver screen: After the hero transforms, they race headlong into a rollercoaster ride of danger and exhilaration until the story reaches its climax.

Where Rey's story differs most importantly from the classic monomyth, though, is that, within the context of the movie, she is no one important. Unlike Luke Skywalker, she isn't identified as the son of a Jedi hero, and she isn't shown with a supernatural guardian who has been living nearby. Counter to most myths and stories studied by Campbell, Rey isn't introduced to the audience as "chosen."

The similarities between the two models and Rey's own journey show that the foundation for creating compelling heroes hasn't changed much over the centuries. But the differences prove there is still innovation and excitement to be had as we update our notions of just who those heroes can be. ☻

STAR WARS

THE OFFICIAL MAGAZINE
FEB/MAR 1999

Your essential STAR WARS universe guide

™

FREE EWAN McGREGOR **POSTER**

TERENCE STAMP
Episode I's Chancellor Valorum

SIGHTS UNSEEN
The lost cut of *Star Wars* revealed!

KOO STARK
She was in *Star Wars*.
No, really.

THE NEW OBI–WAN
Crossing sabers with Ewan McGregor

£3.25
NO: 18

TITAN

EWAN McGREGOR
OBI-WAN KENOBI

ISSUE 18
FEB/MAR 1999

The Essential Guide to Droids published by Del Rey, written by Daniel Wallace, with illustrations by Bill Hughes and schematics by Troy Vigil (February)

Star Wars: X-wing Alliance, the fourth game in Lucasarts' X-wing computer game series is released

Star Wars: The Art of Dave Dorman is re-printed by Welcome Rain Publishers (March)

It's a role that would daunt any actor: following on from the formidable Sir Alec Guinness in a role that everybody knows and loves. Yet Scottish actor Ewan McGregor jumped at the chance to step into Sir Alec's robes as Obi-Wan Kenobi—presumably after they'd been retrieved from the Death Star and cleaned of a certain Sith boot print.

McGregor's performance is often cited as one of the highlights of the prequel trilogy, and in this vintage interview from 1999 he reveals a cheeky sense of humor as he relays how he rose to that seemingly impossible challenge!
—**Jonathan Wilkins**

Ewan Gordon McGregor OBE (born March 31, 1971) was best known for playing Mark Renton in Trainspotting *(1996) before being cast as Obi-Wan Kenobi in* Star Wars. *He has received Golden Globe nominations for Best Actor for* Moulin Rouge! *(2001) and* Salmon Fishing in the Yemen *(2011), and has served as an ambassador for UNICEF U.K. since 2004.*

Portrait of the

JEDI

as a young man

Episode I's Obi-Wan Kenobi tells us about stepping into Sir Alec Guinness' shoes

by Scott Chernoff

Ewan McGregor prefers not to analyse his character. "He's a decent, good guy – one of the good guys," the Scottish actor permits. "He seems to be quite a centred person, and always just slightly behind Liam Neeson most of the time."

But the actor does elaborate – a bit – on what it is to be a Jedi. "They frown a bit, and they're good fighters," he says. "They're the good guys – they stand for everything that's good." Of the relationship between his character and Neeson's, McGregor allows, "Nobody frowns better than me and Liam in this movie, because we have the Jedi frown. We're just kind of cool geezers."

But the casual, flip responses by the 27-year-old McGregor, the ultra-cool icon of the independent film scene thanks to his performances in films like *Trainspotting* and *Velvet Goldmine*, belie not only the size and power of the role he's tackled but also his very real excitement at having won it.

"It was extraordinary to stand in front of the mirror with my wardrobe on," he says. "Because I *was* Obi-Wan Kenobi."

Yes, Ewan McGregor *is* Obi-Wan Kenobi, stepping into the robes and sandals of the legendary Sir Alec Guinness, who defined the role of the stoic sage with a storied past in *Star Wars*, *The Empire Strikes Back*, and *Return of the Jedi*. And rest assured, those robes do not hang lightly. Says the actor, "To be a part of a legend, to be a part of a modern myth, and to play the young Alec Guinness is an incredible honour."

Although he's known for his dark, edgy parts in films like *Shallow Grave* and *A Life Less Ordinary*, McGregor – a full-fledged member of the *Star Wars* Generation – says he jumped at the chance to play Obi-Wan. "A soon as I heard there might be a possibility, it became a kind of mission, because of what *Star Wars* meant to me as a kid. I was six when the first one came out, so they are more than just movies to me."

Gazing around the Episode I set at Leavesden Studios, McGregor adds, "To be walking around here now is quite astonishing to me."

To be sure, it's a long way from the small town of Crieff, Scotland, where he was born, leaving at age 16 to study acting. These days, the actor with the bad boy image is a happy family man who lives in London with his wife, production designer Eve Mouvrakis, and their young

daughter Clara. But still, McGregor remembers his *Star Wars*-infused childhood. "I wasn't fanatical, but I loved the movies – I used to know all the lines to the first one," he says, admitting, "I suppose that is quite fanatical, isn't it – knowing every line."

McGregor allows that his love of the original trilogy may have something to do with the little fact that his uncle, acclaimed actor Denis Lawson, is in all three films. "My uncle Denis played Wedge," Ewan says. "He's so unimpressed with the whole thing it's funny. He came up one day to the set, and as we were walking across the canteen to George, he said, 'He's wearing the same shirt. He's wearing exactly the same shirt he was when he directed the first one.'"

But despite his Force-laden family ties, McGregor insists he was drawn to the *Star Wars* saga because of the power of its stories. "They were like fairy tale movies," he says. "They were completely engrossing. When you watch them as a child, they take over. I used to play *Star Wars* all the time – now they're paying me to do it!"

Indeed, McGregor says he does feel like a kid when he's on the Episode I set. "The first time I was here, I was amazed at how many people were walking around," he says. "In every area you went, there seemed to be about 300 people working away. I was first of all taken with the scale of the thing. I couldn't imagine how big it was.

"And then the props," he continues. "That's something I am familiar with because it's from the *Star Wars* world, so it was incredible to see them all. I was actually screaming out loud! There were about 50 guys working in this prop room, and I was screaming, 'Whoa! Whoa!' But they looked at me as if they understood, so it was alright."

McGregor soon realised that props were just the tip of the iceberg. "Then I met R2-D2 for the first time," he remembers, "which was quite a moment. It was a bit like meeting the Queen – it was a very honoured moment. He kind of just wheeled on set casually, and I swear all the actors were standing around him in a circle going, 'Hey, Artoo!'"

Jokes the star, "Thank God there were no stormtroopers there, or I would have been out of control. I always wanted to be in a stormtrooper outfit. They're the sexiest uniform that's ever been in movies. It's the

> **"I love owning my lightsaber. It's the most exciting thing I've ever known, to have my own lightsaber. I can't have it in my hand and not give it a few twirls."**

best-looking thing ever, the stormtrooper. Maybe they'll be coming up in Episode II or III, so let's just see if I can contain myself."

It's a feeling the actor gets often on the *Star Wars* set. "I love owning my lightsaber," he says. "It's the most exciting thing I've ever known, to have my own lightsaber. I can't have it in my hand and not give it a few twirls."

Declares the actor, "Every day has a *Star Wars* moment or two where you go, 'My God – I'm in *Star Wars*!' Every day."

ever, Obi-Wan is a character with whom audiences are already familiar, and central to McGregor's challenge was making sure his Kenobi could believably become Guinness' Jedi – and, perhaps more importantly, fulfill fans' visions of the Rebel hero as a young man.

"That was the challenge, really," McGregor says, "more than who the Jedi are or what makes

Still, the lifelong love of *Star Wars* that inspired McGregor to aggressively pursue the Obi-Wan role also made the road ahead a daunting one. "It was really scary," says the man who has portrayed everything on screen from a tuba player to a kidnapper to a heroin addict. "The night before, I couldn't sleep. It's probably the thought of sitting in a theatre somewhere and seeing it for the first time, and seeing what we're pretending to do. I can't imagine what I'll be like. It will be nerve-wracking. It will be the most nervous I've been.

"When we did the read-through," he admits, "I was terrified. Before read-throughs, I always imagine I'll do it and then people will say, 'Look, I'm sorry Ewan, but this just isn't going to work out.' But that didn't happen." Instead, the first cast read-through of the script proved to be the beginning of a relaxed and happy shoot. "I thought it would be a massive read-through with all the heads of the department, maybe 200 people sitting and watching. But that wasn't the case – it was very casual."

The pace soon quickened. "This place was buzzing before we started filming," the actor says. "You could feel it as soon as you walked in. There are hundreds of us here. They're a great bunch of people. We all went away together to Africa, and it's always great to go away and get together. We work ridiculously long hours, but we love it. Nobody would be anywhere else. I'll sit in here sometimes and play backgammon after work because I don't want to leave."

But while McGregor's childlike enthusiasm for *Star Wars* never left him, he still approached the part of Ben Kenobi with the same focus and thoughtfulness that he applies to every role. Unlike his past parts, how-

him tick. The step between the end of Episode III and the beginning of Episode IV has to be one that you can believe. It's a leap of faith that I become him, so I worked very hard on trying to get the voice right. I've been doing a lot of dialogue coaching to try and get a younger-sounding version of his voice. It's quite a trick to try to imagine what it sounded like, because in a lot of his younger films he's playing with an accent anyway.

"I watched a lot of his early stuff," the actor continued, "to see what he was like as a young man, and I studied him in *Star Wars*. It's important that we match somehow. I'm always watching him in the first one, the scene in his house where he shows Luke his laser sword for the first time. He's got such a specific voice, the Obi-Wan voice we know, as we associate with an older man, kind of a fatherly voice. There's something really paternal about him, quite calming. He knows what he's about. He's been sitting in the desert for a long time sorting himself out, so I think he's very centred. I'm now going to have to start growing a gray beard, I think."

There were other challenges to wearing the Kenobi cloak – literally. "It's so huge," McGregor says of his Jedi robe. "You're always falling over it. Fighting in it, my sword's going up my sleeve and under my cloak. It looks great, and it's a great idea on paper, but it's pretty hard to wear."

Still, robe problems aside, McGregor says the lightsaber battles in Episode I are "really cool. I think the

fighting in this film is much grungier than the stuff in the first three. It's slightly more aggressive, more ferocious, and faster. They're going to beef it up a bit from the other movies. I think it's rather quite violent, quite tasty fighting."

McGregor says the intensity of the duels makes perfect sense. "There's a lot of talk in Episodes IV, V, and VI about what the Jedi used to be like, and yet you never know what they're really about," he explains. "So you see us kick some butt in this film. I mean, we're jumping all over the place. So it's great to go back and see what everyone was talking about. Why was everyone banging on about the Jedi? Here, we're showing the world what we can do."

Although he's fought and even fenced in other projects, McGregor says his work for Episode I, for which he trained intensively with Stunt Coordinator Nick Gillard, is "not like any fighting I've done before. It's lightsaber fighting – it's a skill of its own. I get to be flash. When I'm fighting, I do lots of twists and spins and twirls and showing off a bit. I've been doing a lot of work on it. Every job you do requires you learning some new skill – it's one of the nicest things about what I do."

But his skills were put to the test when it came time to move from the training mats to principal photography.

Actor Ewan McGregor takes a brief break between shooting on Stage A at Leavesden Studios.

… McGregor says the most powerful special effect was created not by ILM but by a higher authority. *"Tunisia,"* he says, *"is so mind-blowing and huge, it kind of puts you in your place…"*

"It's easier to just go with it when you're not on the set," McGregor confesses. "When you're on the set, suddenly you remember there's 150 people who've come to watch, which makes you nervous. You want to be flash doing it – that's very important to me. Nick's perfect because he'll really egg you on to get them right. The fights will be great."

In addition to mastering the art of the lightsaber, McGregor also had to contend with the most extensive use of blue-screen technology ever put to film, which meant that he spent much of the shoot reacting to elements that would be added to the film later. "Playing off things that

unfazed by the sandstorm. "George said, 'Oh, this is a good omen.' And we said, 'What?!' But he said, 'Oh, this happened in the first one, and this is a good thing that we've had our set destroyed.'

"And everyone just carried on," he continues. "I would have thought on a film like this they would go, 'OK, filming is stopped for two days while we fix everything – everyone just lie by the pool.' But we solved the problem by

aren't there is quite tough," he says. "It's more a technical exercise – making sure you're all looking at the same point, although it's just a point in the air. It's a rather slow and laborious process."

Initially, he found most of the special effects fascinating, but McGregor says he soon stopped trying to figure out how all the state-of-the-art equipment worked. "I'm kind of confused about the ILM guys," he says. "I'll ask, 'What does that do?' Someone will explain it, and my mind will just go. I'll switch off and then at the end I'll go, 'Oh, right.' Because I can't understand. I don't need to either. It's so confusing I don't even bother to ask anymore."

But McGregor says the most powerful special effect was created not by ILM but by a higher authority. "Tunisia," he says, "is so mind-blowing and huge, it kind of puts you in your place," and that was especially true the day a gigantic sandstorm hit the area, wiping out most of the Episode I sets. "Seeing that was quite extraordinary," he says. "I've never witnessed anything like it. We saw this wall of sand coming toward us – from the comfort of the hotel I have to say, not from the desert. It hit us and the lightning was going across the sky. It was awesome, amazing."

When he showed up at the hard-hit *Star Wars* location after the storm, McGregor was happily surprised to learn that the show was going on. "I thought it was really exciting, and it was great to see Rick McCallum," he says. "He's such a producer, he was running around – he was just kind of in his element, and we were going to carry on filming."

In fact, McGregor says director George Lucas was completely

filming somewhere else that hadn't been damaged so much while everyone patched up the damage. And everyone did. The crew pulls together because they're a brilliant crew."

McGregor says the laid back response to natural disaster was typical of the director. "He just deals with everything as it comes, and with a sense of childlike excitement about it," he says. "He's very straightforward. In terms of fights, when it comes to blocking, he's so inventive on his feet. But on the whole he knows exactly what every frame of the film is going to look like.

"I like him a lot. I like working with him because he lets you get on with it. He's cast us all because we can get on with it, really, without him having to worry about us too much. If you do something he doesn't like, he tells you, but on the whole you just crack on with it."

Lucas isn't the only member of the Episode I team that McGregor admires. The actor says he never expected to be so impressed with his young co-star Jake Lloyd, who was eight-years-old when he filmed his part as the

photo: Keith Hamshere

Episode I Stunt Coordinator Nick Gillard shares a light moment with actor Ewan McGregor just prior to a heavy-duty stunt on the Flight Shed 1 stage at Leavesden Studios.

young Anakin Skywalker. "I've never worked with a kid actor as good as Jake, ever," McGregor says. "Jake is just phenomenal. I've never once heard him complain. I find myself saying, 'How many takes are we going to do on this scene,' and then I look at him and suddenly I feel ashamed because he's never complained at all.

"He pulls your pants off with his jokes and stories," McGregor continues. "He's very good fun to have around. I really enjoy him a lot, and he's brilliant. It seems to be really good, the work he's doing."

Jake's youth is also an echo of Ewan's when he first became enchanted with the *Star Wars* saga. "I felt really different about playing this role," the actor says. "Most of the films I've made so far, my daughter can't watch because they're full of heroin and needles. And that's the really important thing about *Star Wars*. They're for children. It's about love and peace and warfare and the people. It's a fairy tale – princesses and princes and good and evil.

"Fairy tales are so important for kids. Because I grew up with that, I read them to my daughter. Some people don't. A lot of people have stopped, and so nursery rhymes and fairy tales have stopped. The kids don't know what that is. So in a way, if this replaces that, then I'm really happy to be part of it. I love kids, and I remember how it felt watching *Star Wars* when I was six, and for my daughter to be able to sit and watch this with me in it…"

Ewan McGregor pauses, contemplating that moment. "I don't know quite what she'll make of that," he says, smiling. "We'll ask her later, in a couple of years." ☻

Additional reporting by Lynne Hale and David West Reynolds

STAR WARS

INSIDER ®

ISSUE #159
U.S. $7.99
CAN $9.99
AUG/SEPT 2015

TITAN

MIDI-CHLORIANS
A CLOSER LOOK

ISSUE 159
AUG/SEP 2015

The inaugural Force Friday event takes place on September 4th, launching the run up to the release of *The Force Awakens*

Star Wars: Absolutely Everything You Need to Know by Adam Bray, Kerrie Dougherty, Cole Horton, and Michael Kogge published by DK (September)

Star Wars: Aftermath by Chuck Wendig, published by Del Rey (September)

The Weapon of a Jedi: A Luke Skywalker Adventure, a junior novel by Jason Fry released by Disney Lucasfilm Press (September)

Midi-Chlorians were a controversial addition to *Star Wars* mythology, so I was keen to examine them in the pages of *Insider*. As passionate an advocate of frank discussion as you could hope to meet, writer Dan Zehr was perfect for the task and compiled a truly riveting and insightful examination of one of the saga's most misunderstood concepts.—**Jonathan Wilkins**

UNDER THE MICROSCOPE:
A CLOSER LOOK AT

THEY ARE THE MYSTERIOUS CREATURES
WHOSE PRESENCE SIGNIFIES A BEING'S
CONNECTION TO THE FORCE, BUT IS
THERE MORE TO THE MIDI-CHLORIANS
THAN MEETS THE EYE?
WORDS: DAN ZEHR

MIDI-CHLORIANS

1999 was a banner year for *Star Wars* fans, as it saw the release of a brand new film, *The Phantom Menace.* The first installment of the prequel trilogy brought us many wonderful new characters, planets, and events that added to the tapestry of our beloved saga. Finally, the story of Anakin Skywalker would be told.

However, one scene in particular took fandom by storm, as it introduced the polarizing term, "midi-chlorians." Once Jedi Master Qui-Gon Jinn initiated the idea of midi-chlorians to Anakin Skywalker, the questions began: What are midi-chlorians, and what do they mean for *Star Wars*? Is the Force biological or genetic? What about the spiritual aspects of the Force? Why aren't midi-chlorians mentioned in the original trilogy?

UNDER THE MICROSCOPE

A closer examination of what midi-chlorians are reveals a fascinating, complex concept that beautifully blends many aspects of mythological, spiritual, and biological constructs into one term.

The first time audiences learned of the existence of the Force, Obi-Wan Kenobi explained to a young Luke Skywalker, "The Force is what gives a Jedi his power; it's an energy field created by all things. It surrounds us, penetrates us, binds the galaxy together." Based on this explanation, the Force, from its onset, was not purely spiritual; all things create it. This beautiful description of the harmony and balance of the Force has biological implications as well.

Many audience members (myself included) did not immediately grasp the organic nature of the Force, but George Lucas had a cooperative, balanced idea in mind all along. George Lucas once told noted *Star Wars* author J. W. Rinzler:

"I'm assuming that the midi-chlorians are a race that everybody knows about [in the world of *Star Wars*]. The way you interact and interface with this larger energy field [the Force] is through the midi-chlorians, which are sensitive to the energy. They are at the core of your life, which is the cell, the living cell. They are in a symbiotic relationship with the cell. And then, because they're all interconnected as one, they can communicate with the larger Force field. That's how you deal with the Force."

Qui-Gon Jinn explained midi-chlorians to Anakin Skywalker as, "... a microscopic life form that resides within all living cells. Without the midi-chlorians, life could not exist, and we would have no knowledge of the Force. They continually speak to us, telling us the will of the Force."

Insider asked four *Star Wars* experts their opinion of what midi-chlorians are: Kyle Newman (director of *Fanboys*), Ian Doescher (author of *William Shakespeare's Star Wars* series), Paul McDonald (author of *The Star Wars Heresies*), and Cory Clubb (co-host of the *Coffee With Kenobi* podcast).

HOW DO YOU EXPLAIN MIDI-CHLORIANS?

Kyle Newman: I love midi-chlorians. Despite their biological explanation in *The Phantom Menace*, they still exist on a spiritual level. Just because the Jedi can quantify them doesn't remove the magic from the topic. The midi-chlorians are merely a conduit into this great and wondrous energy field. They are *not* the Force itself; they're just a way to commune with it or tap into it.

Luke reaches the apex of potential because of his hereditary line. Many revered it, respected it (Ackbar says, "May the Force be with you," along with others), but none could even come close to harnessing its unique attributes other than a chosen few. It's extremely clear that Luke, and subsequently Leia, are special because of their genetics.

Ian Doescher: Honestly, I try not to, but if I had to, I would probably say midi-chlorians are a life-form/life-force that live in all things (kind of like atoms) and imbue all things with energy or, if you will, with the Force.

Paul McDonald: Fortunately, Qui-Gon's speech to Anakin in *The Phantom Menace* is the perfect jumping off point for any discussion about this. At no point are the midi-chlorians and the Force said to be interchangeable, and they bear much the same relationship as a radio merely picking up a radio signal. Midi-chlorians are the conduits, the bridge, to that mystical energy field we've been hearing about since the 1970s, not a contradiction of it. They are no more the Force than the speakers are the music they broadcast.

Cory Clubb: Something inside Luke harnessed him to take down the Death Star.

Was it the courage he lacked or the privilege of Ben Kenobi's mentorship? Further still, Yoda invokes these same mysteries on Dagobah, and we as viewers just believe his wisdom and know what he says and does is possible in the fact that Yoda himself understands it. Fast forward to Qui-Gon Jinn's blood sample, and it may break down to something as simple as a test done for a newborn baby.

HOW DO MIDI-CHLORIANS ENHANCE THE MYTHOS?

KN: From a storytelling/filmmaking standpoint, it feels like George Lucas included the notion of midi-chlorians so there was a quantifiable way to both recognize and justify Anakin to the Council. After all, the boy is a slave child outside of the Jedi normal search patterns, and a fatherless Force mystery.

I always assumed that the Empire collected or destroyed much of this information and tech, further submerging the Jedi into myth. By eradicating their central temple, the Emperor went right to the heart. The Jedi's entire infrastructure, their ability to locate and train future generations, was completely destroyed. It was akin to the razing of the Alexandrian Library—one can only conjecture how much knowledge was lost.

ID: The big question when *The Phantom Menace* came out was, do we really need midi-chlorians? Did we need an explanation of what makes the Force what it is?

I think midi-chlorians enhance the mythology of *Star Wars* primarily because they help build the *Star Wars* universe—they expand it and add to our understanding of it. I was recently on a convention panel about

how, as an author, you create a world; having more information about midi-chlorians adds to the world George Lucas created.
PM: *The Phantom Menace* is perhaps the most deliberate example of this. Qui-Gon defines symbiosis as "life forms living together for mutual advantage." This theme runs like a thread throughout the film, whether it is on the planetary scale of the Naboo and the Gungans learning to work together, or the microscopic one of the midi-chlorians and the Force likewise communicating.

In *Ethics for a New Millennium,* the Dalai Lama states that when the lens of symbiosis is taken up, "We begin to see that the universe we inhabit can be understood in terms of a living organism where each cell works in balanced cooperation with every other cell to sustain the whole."

So symbiosis is perhaps *the* theme of *Star Wars,* and George Lucas provided a solid, concrete metaphor through the midi-chlorians.
CC: How do books help us to understand, rather than folk tales or storied wisdom? Books are physical and we can take the knowledge and go on; wisdom, likewise, is profitable to experience, but is skewed to one's opinion. Which enhances our existence more? Neither. We go on regardless, thus if another aspect of the Force was revealed, would it change our experience? I'm not sure midi-chlorians enhance the mythology of *Star Wars* or not, but [they do] raise more questions to our own understanding of how the Force works in the *Star Wars* universe.

> ## "I THINK MIDI-CHLORIANS ENHANCE THE MYTHOLOGY OF *STAR WARS,* PRIMARILY BECAUSE THEY HELP EXPAND IT AND ADD TO OUR UNDERSTANDING OF IT."—IAN DOESCHER

CAN MIDI-CHLORIANS BE BOTH BIOLOGICAL AND SPIRITUAL?

KN: Some complain that there was no mention of midi-chlorians in the original trilogy, so their existence in the prequels is unnecessary… but in fact there was *no need* for midi-chlorians in the original trilogy. Did Obi-Wan *need* to give Luke a blood test the same way Qui-Gon took Anakin's? No, Luke was a known quantity he had been overseeing his whole life and the descendent of the Chosen One, whereas Anakin was a complete enigma to Qui-Gon—a vergence. And furthermore, since *The Phantom Menace* is the first part of a much larger, ever-expanding saga, the foundations needed to be established.
ID: I don't pretend to be an expert in midi-chlorians, so my immediate answer to this question is: Aren't we? Humans are embodied, fleshy stuff—we're highly functioning animals, but still biological animals. Yet, we're also spiritual beings —whether religious or not, each of us

is spiritual in some way and approaches the world with our spiritual selves just as much as with our physical selves. If we can do it, why can't midi-chlorians?
PM: Curiously, this is another unique spin in the *Star Wars* saga. In this particular mythology, the spiritual is the offspring of the biological world. Physical life is the very root of it, the thing that causes it to grow and expand. Not to mention the fact that it has been established since the original trilogy that Force ability is passed down through families and bloodlines, so it only makes sense that there would be a certain connection between the two, as opposed to an antagonism. This is summed up rather tellingly in *The Power of Myth.* In the words of Joseph Campbell, who was an enormous influence on George Lucas, "Spiritual life is the bouquet, the perfume, the flowering and fulfillment of a human life, not a supernatural virtue imposed upon it." And that's exactly what the Force is. That the biological and the mystical can find a common ground, with one a potential ladder leading to the other, can be seen as quite spiritual indeed.
CC: As human beings we strive to understand, and in doing so, we want proof,

but yet we also have the ability to understand things that are greater or beyond ourselves. Our capacity to have a foot in both the spiritual realm as well as the physical, personifies our diversity and connection to one another. I see this as the same way with midi-chlorians; they exist by way of understanding. It's not that midi-chlorians are the Force itself, but that they are vessels of it in physical form. Not parasites, but something like fireflies attracted to light or more simply, wind in a bird's feathers. Imagine for just a moment if Yoda had done a midi-chlorian test on Luke, would that have told him different about Luke's ability in the Force?

NOT CRUDE MATTER

Yoda famously stated on Dagobah, "Luminous beings are we. Not this crude matter," and demonstrated more fully the biological and spiritual connection that the Force contains. His journey through season six of *The Clone Wars* verified the association as well. In fact, Yoda's teachings also echo that of a Buddhist

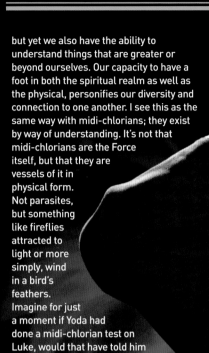

belief: Praying before a meal changes the molecular makeup, making it more wholesome and nutritious. There are cultural implications for the spiritual aspect of things changing the biological chemistry of something. The likely truth of this fully forms Lucas's concept of midi-chlorians, and we are left with a richer, more intriguing, understanding of the Force.

Midi-chlorians are a paradoxical blend of the organic and spiritual; they are a combination of the best of both worlds,

coalescing ideologies from various cultures and religious beliefs into a cohesive blend of faith, genetics, and biology. Further reflection and analysis of midi-chlorians invites much discussion; all the more reason to embrace the mythology that George Lucas created.

This page: Anakin Skywalker boasted the highest known midi-chlorian count.

44

THE ESSENTIAL *STAR WARS: THE FORCE AWAKENS* COLLECTIBLES!

THE JEDI REVEALED: SECRETS OF THE FORCE EXPLORED

STAR WARS

INSIDER

START WARS!

TAKE ARMS!
TAKE AIM!
TAKE NO PRISONERS!

STAR WARS
BATTLEFRONT
EA

IS HERE!

PLUS:
AN EXCLUSIVE
TIE-IN STORY!

ISSUE #161
US $7.99
CAN $9.99
NOV/DEC 2015

TITAN

SIR ALEC GUINNESS
OBI-WAN KENOBI

ISSUE 161
NOV/DEC 2015

LEGO *Star Wars: Small Scenes from a Big Galaxy* by Vesa Lehtimäki, published by DK (November)

Star Wars: Shattered Empire trade paperback published by Marvel Comics. Written by Greg Rucka, with art by Marco Checcetto, Angel Unzueta, and Emilio Laiso (November)

Star Wars: Battlefront, developed by DICE, is released by Electronic Arts (November)

Star Wars: The Force Awakens is released in theatres on December 18th

For a character killed off midway through the first *Star Wars* movie, Obi-Wan Kenobi is certainly popular. In many ways he is the spiritual center of the original trilogy, as he guides Luke on his path to becoming a Jedi and offers some (it has to be said, slightly questionable) advice from the netherworld.

Trica Barr's in-depth feature examines his role in the narrative and why he is so beloved by fans, despite his failings.

As an added bonus, we present some words from Sir Alec Guinness himself, as he reflects on the making of *Star Wars* and working with George Lucas.—**Jonathan Wilkins**

Sir Alec Guinness CH CBE (born April 2, 1914, died August 5, 2000) began his career on the stage, before finding fame in a run of Ealing Studios comedies, including Kind Hearts and Coronets (1949), *in which he played eight different characters, and* The Ladykillers (1955). *His celebrated collaborations with director David Lean include* Great Expectations *(1946),* Oliver Twist *(1948),* The Bridge on the River Kwai *(1957),* Lawrence of Arabia *(1962),* Doctor Zhivago *(1965), and* A Passage to India *(1984). He won the Academy Award for Best Actor for his role in* The Bridge on the River Kwai *and was nominated as Best Supporting Actor for* Star Wars.

In 1959, he was knighted by Queen Elizabeth II for services to the arts. He received a star on the Hollywood Walk of Fame in 1960, the Academy Honorary Award for lifetime achievement in 1980, and the BAFTA Academy Fellowship Award in 1989.

A KNIGHT'S TALE

OBI-WAN KENOBI COULD HAVE CHOSEN TO TELL LUKE THE TRUTH ABOUT HIS FATHER. HE COULD HAVE REFUSED TO TRAIN ANAKIN, OR TOLD THE JEDI COUNCIL THEY WERE WRONG TO ORDER HIS FRIEND TO SPY ON PALPATINE. DESPITE HIS FAILINGS, OBI-WAN REMAINS A BELOVED CHARACTER. IN HER ONGOING SERIES ABOUT HEROES AND THEIR JOURNEYS THROUGH STORIES, TRICIA BARR EXAMINES THE REASONS BEHIND HIS POPULARITY ACROSS GENERATIONS OF FANDOM.

The heroes of modern myth rarely go it alone. Sidekicks, mentors, peers, friends, and family may accompany the hero on a quest or weave in and out of a tale, each of them helping to shape the course of the hero's path. I have explained my theory on character interaction this way: Each character possesses his or her own gravity; if a hero is a comet rocketing through space, then every other mass in their proximity will affect the trajectory. Greg Weisman, the *Star Wars Rebels* season one showrunner and writer of the fantastic *Kanan* comic series, well-renowned for his heroic ensemble storytelling, agreed enthusiastically with this theory in an interview for the Fangirls Going Rogue podcast. In the six *Star Wars* saga films to date, no other character has exerted as much gravitational pull on the parallel heroic journeys as Obi-Wan Kenobi.

For the prequel trilogy, Anakin is the missile propelled on an adventure. As he vectors through the galaxy far, far away, we observe his trajectory affected by Padmé Amidala, perhaps a beautiful moon; Qui-Gon Jinn, the Alderaan whose gravity suddenly disappears; Obi-Wan, a sizeable planet; and Darth Sidious, the black hole sucking everything toward its event horizon. While Palpatine has the most significant impact on Anakin's journey, successfully reversing his triumphant flight path, the hero who accompanies young Skywalker through most of his adventure is Obi-Wan, his mentor and ultimately a peer and friend. Yet Obi-Wan has retained his status among fans as a beloved hero in spite of his role in Anakin's tragic fall. We can find the explanation in his humble origins as the hermit in *A New Hope*.

Though he affects the path of Luke to almost the same extent, this time Obi-Wan exerts his gravity through wiser and nobler archetypes.

MYTH-MAKING IN THE *STAR WARS* GALAXY

From the beginning, *Star Wars* excelled at the basic tools of storytelling. The franchise is heralded as groundbreaking, generally in terms of its visual effects and sound, but the movies also evolved storytelling in new and unexpected ways.

In particular, *Star Wars* built upon and expanded the notions of teamwork in stories that had

---

OBI-WAN HAS RETAINED HIS STATUS AMONG FANS AS A BELOVED HERO, DESPITE HIS ROLE IN ANAKIN'S TRAGIC FALL.

come before. *Lord of the Rings* has the Fellowship of the Ring; in *The Lion, The Witch and The Wardrobe* the Pevensie sisters and brothers work together to save Narnia. The ever-popular *The Wizard of Oz* follows Dorothy on her journey to find home, and in achieving her goal, her band of traveling companions gain their own personal victories: courage for the Cowardly Lion, a heart for the Tin Man, and a brain for the Scarecrow. Yet like Aragorn's rise to the throne at the culmination of Frodo's quest in *The Lord of the Rings*, their personal triumphs occur as part of a story that begins by setting Dorothy's goals. By contrast, *A New Hope* opens by establishing a broader set of goals for the Rebel Alliance, with a princess and stolen engineering plans in immediate peril. Ultimately, it is Luke the dreamer who gets the adventure he hopes for, and achieves the rebels' goal by blowing up the Death Star.

While *A New Hope* capitalized on the popular ingrained understanding of the monomyth (a.k.a the hero's journey), the movie about Luke Skywalker's heroic rise also propelled other characters in his team to meteoric heights. One need look no further than the Celebration Anaheim crowd's reaction to Han's, "Chewie, we're home," or the social media response in the days following Comic-Con International: San Diego's first behind-the-scenes images of Carrie Fisher filming a scene as Leia to recognize how important all three legacy characters are to the fandom. Then there is Obi-Wan Kenobi, whose mythic standing and popularity over the years has never waned, but instead continued to go from strength to strength.

THE 1977 AUDIENCE ACCEPTED THE NOBILITY OF OBI-WAN KENOBI WHILE THEIR IMAGINATIONS BEGAN TO PONDER THE HERITAGE AND SIGNIFICANCE OF A KNIGHT LEADING A SOLITARY LIFE

This distinction from prior stories offers the framework for a tale about a Chosen One's journey that creates multiple heroes with and their own distinctive trajectories, their own gravities that influence the conclusion of their shared story.

THE EVERYMAN AND THE NOBILITY

Many notable heroic archetypes can exist as a central protagonist or alongside a main hero. In *Star Wars Insider* Issue 158, I compared *A New Hope*'s Han Solo to *The Wizard of Oz*'s Tin Man, both Accidental Heroes. Harrison Ford has played other archetypes, too, such as Indiana Jones the Bold Adventurer, a heroic model suited to a story more about excitement and less about self-discovery. Nonetheless *Indiana Jones and The Last Crusade* nudged the archaeology professor with a propensity for adventure into new heroic territory by introducing his father to the tale, thereby creating a story about conflict of a more personal nature, one of family and self. Also within *Last Crusade* is another easily recognizable heroic archetype: the Knight. Across literature Knights are revered for their code of honor and sense of duty. *Last Crusade*'s Knight guarded the Holy Grail for 700 years. Obi-Wan Kenobi's devotion didn't reach quite that magnitude, having spent slightly under two decades protecting Luke Skywalker, but

orbit hints at the strength of Luke's gravity as a character. Yet it is Obi-Wan's ability to relate easily to the everyman, Chewbacca and Han Solo, that provides a clue to the characteristic that has endeared him to the masses: his humanity.

Imbued with noble qualities and humble everyman touches, Kenobi transitions through Episode IV's first act into another archetype—that of the Wizard. While wizards are often identified by their exceptional skills with magical powers, such as Gandalf in *Lord of the Rings*, the Merriam-Webster dictionary's first definition is "wise man." Pop culture has seen an influx of less magical, but wiser wizards, from *The Avengers'* Nick Fury to *The Hunger Games'* Haymitch. Notably, both of these modern-day wizards mentor teams rather than just individuals. Fury and Haymitch also have pushed the wizard into more complex moral territory with their actions, revealing the characters as flawed, or perhaps more human.

George Lucas' clever remolding of archetypes pushed storytellers to consider the infinite possibilities available alongside a monomyth, as opposed to the narrow window presented in a lone hero's trajectory that resigns non-central characters to a plot-induced fate. Even Chewbacca, the Noble Savage archetype, is given brief but impactful moments of exerting his gravity when a mournful growl or knowing glance serves to nudge Han to make different choices. Over and over, *Star Wars* emphasizes the power of choice over fate, and it has proven that theme can empower its audience.

Clockwise, from left: Obi-Wan negotiates the heroes' escape from Tatooine; the wise Jedi, who continues to look over events even after death; the older Jedi and his young apprentice form a strong bond despite their brief time together; Luke Skywalker learns a valuable lesson about the Force and the weak-minded.

the archetype is so embedded in mythos that it establishes a set of presumed characteristics when introduced in a movie like *A New Hope*.

Once Luke had asked old hermit Ben Kenobi if he had fought in the Clone Wars and he answered, "I was a Jedi Knight, the same as your father," the 1977 audience accepted the nobility of Kenobi while their imaginations began to ponder the heritage and significance of a knight living a solitary life. Kenobi choosing to remain in young Skywalker's

A CERTAIN POINT OF VIEW

IN EPISODE IV, OBI-WAN TURNS FROM WIZARD TO MARTYR OVER THE COURSE OF THE SECOND ACT.

While Obi-Wan began Episode IV in the Knight archetype, he transforms from Wizard to Martyr over the course of the second act. Crafting impactful deaths is an art in and of itself. At times a senseless death can serve a storytelling purpose; it is much harder to piece together events that allow a character to meet death in the manner most humans wish they could, with our wits and grace and in a way that makes a difference. In much the same way Aslan reappears in *The Lion, The Witch and The Wardrobe* to serve as a Savior, providing the heroes with the key to victory, Obi-Wan's disembodied voice offers the last bit of guidance to assist Luke's triumph.

By the time the Victory March plays in *A New Hope*, Luke Skywalker is cemented as a mythic hero for firing a torpedo into a exhaust shaft, a task great pilots thought impossible even with the aid of technology. Why was Luke able to make that odds-defying shot? Because Obi-Wan provided him with the most powerful tool available to humankind—the belief in self.

In the first *Star Wars* movie, Obi-Wan Kenobi's character draws upon many common archetypal elements used across centuries of storytelling, and then shifts between them. Just like the new generation of franchise movie-makers need to study the physical artistry of balancing practical effects and computer-generated graphics, they will also turn a careful eye to the careful balance of character design and then the even more complicated artform of

maintaining the legacy of a character over time. In fact, we can all learn something about storytelling by analyzing Obi-Wan's progression in his numerous roles in the saga, from the wise wizard in *A New Hope* and spectral advisor in *The Empire Strikes Back* and *Return of the Jedi*, to the heroic champion of the prequel trilogy and multi-faceted general in *The Clone Wars*. As a storyteller myself, my takeaway from the character's success is that epic sagas need a non-

protagonist character who represents the values of the storyteller; in *Star Wars*, that is Obi-Wan. Though a person possessing amazing powers, Kenobi embodies the complexities of our own daily human struggle. His Force ability doesn't change the fact that each day he is faced with new choices, sometimes seemingly impossible choices. In each instance, Obi-Wan tries his best to do the right thing, and when he doesn't, he persists until life presents the next opportunity. ☮

From top: Obi-Wan becomes one with the Force; Sir Alec Guinness as Ben (Obi-Wan) Kenobi.

ALEC GUINNESS
AS OBI-WAN KENOBI

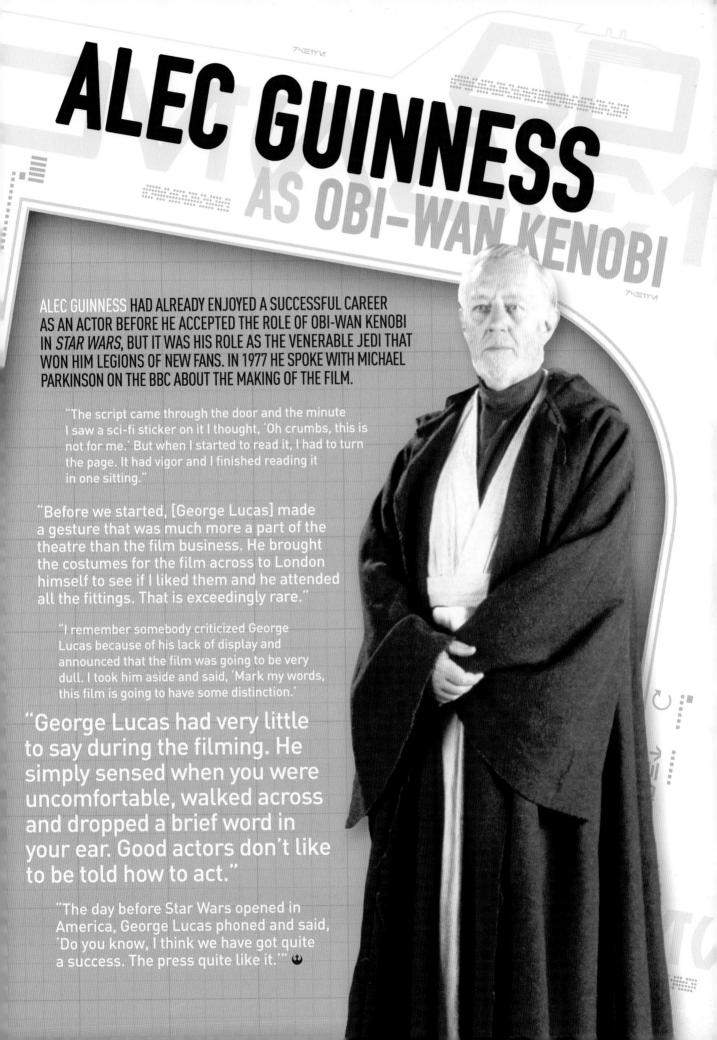

ALEC GUINNESS HAD ALREADY ENJOYED A SUCCESSFUL CAREER AS AN ACTOR BEFORE HE ACCEPTED THE ROLE OF OBI-WAN KENOBI IN *STAR WARS*, BUT IT WAS HIS ROLE AS THE VENERABLE JEDI THAT WON HIM LEGIONS OF NEW FANS. IN 1977 HE SPOKE WITH MICHAEL PARKINSON ON THE BBC ABOUT THE MAKING OF THE FILM.

"The script came through the door and the minute I saw a sci-fi sticker on it I thought, 'Oh crumbs, this is not for me.' But when I started to read it, I had to turn the page. It had vigor and I finished reading it in one sitting."

"Before we started, [George Lucas] made a gesture that was much more a part of the theatre than the film business. He brought the costumes for the film across to London himself to see if I liked them and he attended all the fittings. That is exceedingly rare."

"I remember somebody criticized George Lucas because of his lack of display and announced that the film was going to be very dull. I took him aside and said, 'Mark my words, this film is going to have some distinction.'

"George Lucas had very little to say during the filming. He simply sensed when you were uncomfortable, walked across and dropped a brief word in your ear. Good actors don't like to be told how to act."

"The day before Star Wars opened in America, George Lucas phoned and said, 'Do you know, I think we have got quite a success. The press quite like it.'"

ON YOUR TRAIL!
CREATING THE BOUNTY HUNTERS

ROMANCING A JEDI!
SATINE'S STORY REVEALED

STAR WARS

INSIDER

ISSUE #117
MAY/JUNE 2010
U.S. $5.99 CAN $6.99

THE RETURN OF
BOBA FETT
READY FOR REVENGE!

IVOR BEDDOES
STORYBOARDS

ISSUE 117
MAY/JUNE 2010

Star Wars: The Empire Strikes Back released 30 years ago, on May 21st, 1980

Star Wars: Fate of the Jedi: Allies by Christie Golden, published by Del Rey (May)

Star Wars: The Clone Wars Character Encyclopedia by Jason Fry, published by DK (June)

Star Wars Omnibus: A Long Time Ago.... Volume 1 published by Dark Horse Comics (June)

One of the benefits of *Insider*'s close working relationship with Lucasfilm's publishing arm is the access to bonus material from assorted book projects. Strict page counts can mean projects such as J. W. Rinzler's *The Making of The Empire Strikes Back* simply can't contain all the amazing material, so *Insider* is on hand to provide an appreciative home to the extras—such as these rare storyboards by Ivor Beddoes. A true master of his craft, Beddoes was a real visionary with a distinctive style, and these visualizations show just how much planning and craft goes into planning a scene. It is testament to Beddoes' skill, and that of the entire *Empire* team, that the finished sequence is every bit as thrilling as these gripping storyboards.—**Jonathan Wilkins**

Ivor William Gilmour Beddoes (born April 28, (1909, died March 14, 1981) was a British matte painter, sketch and storyboard artist, costume and set designer, painter, dancer, composer, and poet. He is best known for his painting and illustration work on movies such as The Red Shoes *(1948),* Barry Lyndon *(1975),* Star Wars *(1977), and* Superman the Movie *(1978).*

CONFRONTATION IN CLOUD CITY!
THE FIGHT CONTINUES

The storyboards of Ivor Beddoes.
By J. W. Rinzler

THE STORY SO FAR

Rushing to Cloud City in an attempt to rescue his friends, Luke Skywalker is drawn into a lightsaber duel with Darth Vader. Flung through a window by the Dark Lord, an exhausted Luke searches for a means of escape.

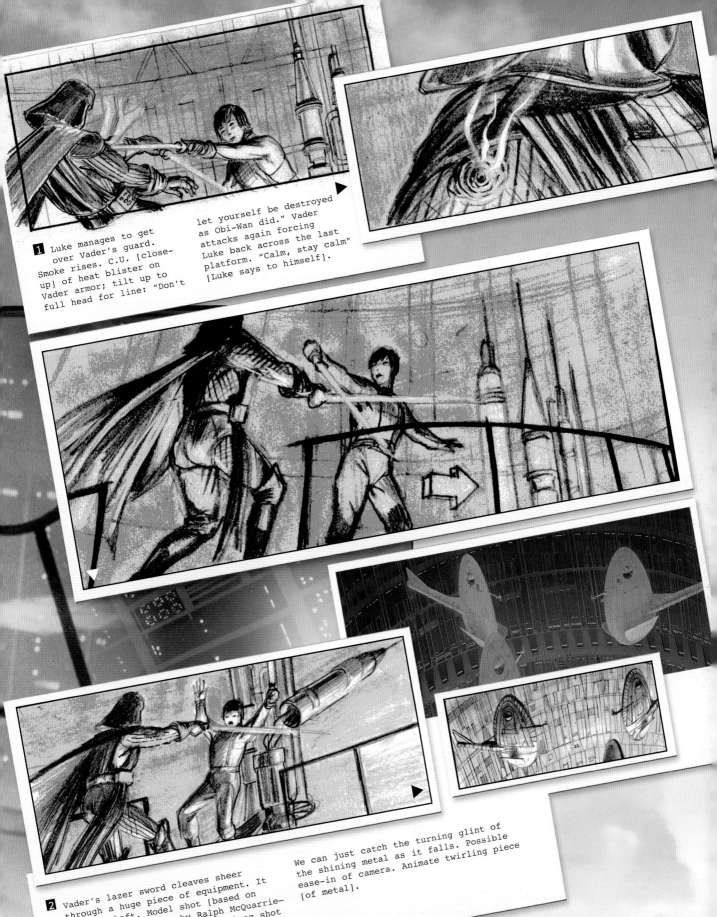

1 Luke manages to get over Vader's guard. Smoke rises. C.U. [close-up] of heat blister on Vader armor; tilt up to full head for line: "Don't let yourself be destroyed as Obi-Wan did." Vader attacks again forcing Luke back across the last platform. "Calm, stay calm" [Luke says to himself].

2 Vader's lazer sword cleaves sheer through a huge piece of equipment. It falls down shaft. Model shot [based on production illustration by Ralph McQuarrie—later shot would be simplified]: long shot of reactor shaft. Luke and Vader are now at the extreme tip of the vast pod.

We can just catch the turning glint of the shining metal as it falls. Possible ease-in of camera. Animate twirling piece [of metal].

3 [NOTE: Storyboard missing for Vader's reveal of fatherhood, for security measures taken at that time. We pick up after Luke has plunged into the reactor shaft.] Diagramatic illustration of camera work for jump method (using black velvets and wide angle lens): A funnel of black velvet; double for Luke on wire up on gantry.
Camera on Nodal Head [special camera gear] so that, as camera pans with Luke sideways and out past camera, the wire is always behind him.

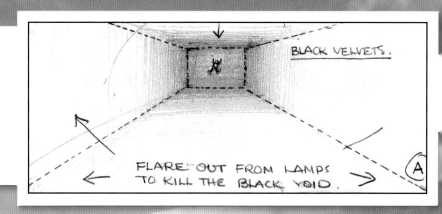

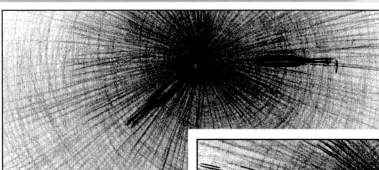

5 Progression of Luke plunging down reactor funnel:
Matte shot of the mile wide funnel from the reactor.

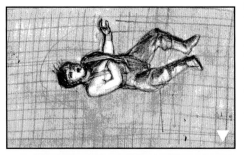

7 Tumbling harness. Luke in free jump to net covered with black velvet. Sound of wind blowing. Free-falling, face down onto net. Luke hits the glass-like wall of the side of the funnel.

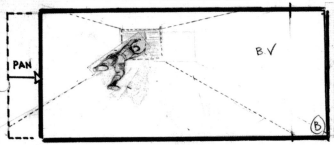
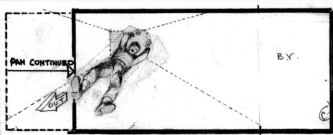

4 Lighting. Luke is hurtling down to the reactor a mile below—the terrific glare blinds out the darkness which Luke is falling toward.

[Camera movement is such that] as Luke is lowered, he arrests speed so that he begins to float (rising wind sound is pushing up at him.) He vanishes from bottom of frame. Stunt double to incline his position as per the camera operator's instructions as Nodal head pans him out of frame.

6 As Luke is shot against black velvet, the tunnel should be kept dark as he is superimposed.
Suddenly Luke reappears—being blown upward.

9 Luke is sliding down the smooth wall-face helplessly. Suddenly he is sucked into an intake ventilation tunnel. C.U.: Vader watching. He turns and exits. It is probably best to shoot this upside down [shot of Luke]: This way Luke would slide "down" (up). He would appear to be sucked in.

8 Diagram of gently inclined plane of polished surface: artist (stuntman) simulates landing against wall—immediately the surface is made steep. Artist slips down. Camera tilts down to follow him. He passes out of frame and lands on boxes.

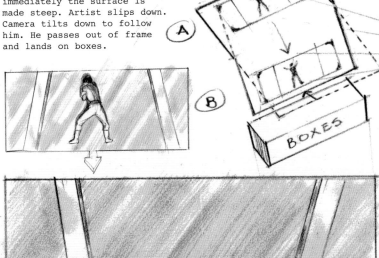

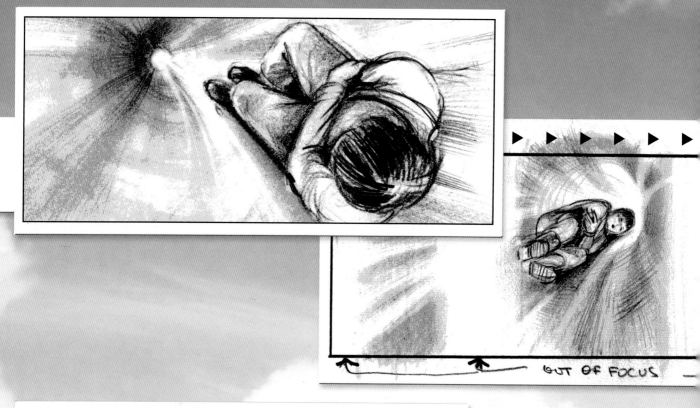

OUT OF FOCUS

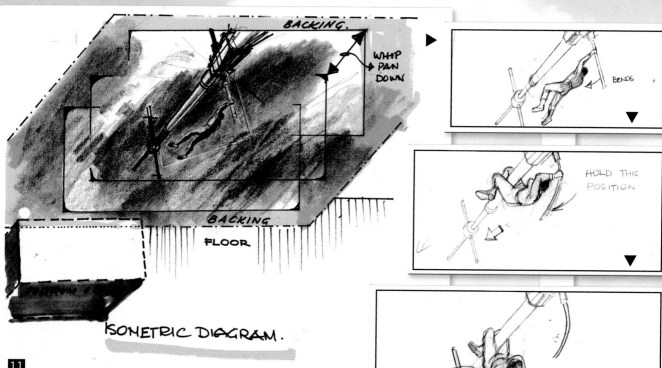

BACKING.

WHIP PAN DOWN

BACKING

FLOOR

ISOMETRIC DIAGRAM.

BENDS

HOLD THIS POSITION

11 Isometric diagram: slowly moving cloud-glass effect on backing. See Ralph color sketch [Mcquarrie's production painting].

12 With a useless arm, Luke has managed to catch on to a penultimate bar projection, which bends under his dead weight (wind is blowing thin clouds past him). Luke manages to hook his legs round the inverted mast—just as his good arm slithers off the tilted bar. He again goes sliding down, falling backward… and finished up really at the end of his escape. His position must seem utterly hopeless.
  Cut into cloud plate close-up with *Millennium Falcon* speeding from distance.

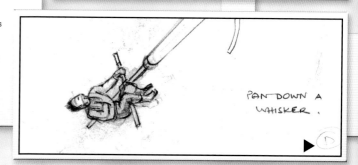

PAN DOWN A WHISKER.

10 A series of shots of Luke sliding away from or towards camera, hugging his injured arm. Luke comes skeetering around a bend. He bursts through the grill, which slows his descent. He drops.

13 As Luke slips down, he wrenches himself round. He is now in a totally impossible position. Somewhere up there is the bottom of Cloud City. (shoot this upside down—gum his hair upright).

Original concept art by Ralph McQuarrie

15 Luke rouses himself by instinct. Then he faints. He falls. His grip goes last so that his legs slither out and drop—his body twists so that he falls feet down and turned toward us.

17 Luke is hanging in harness. Hold on two-shot of Leia and Chewie as Luke vanishes! Long hold—we hear a plop—he is on top! All hell breaks to get up to him. (Discuss action with Kersh.)

14 Extension of Ralph's painting: matte painting of the underside of Cloud City. Angles on Luke nearly unconscious to intercut with *Falcon*. Shot of the *Falcon* coming in—fast.

16 The Falcon streaks through camera. POV from the *Falcon*. Model Luke falling—new position as a figure veers by wind forces.

18

[The *Falcon* flies away, having rescued Luke.]

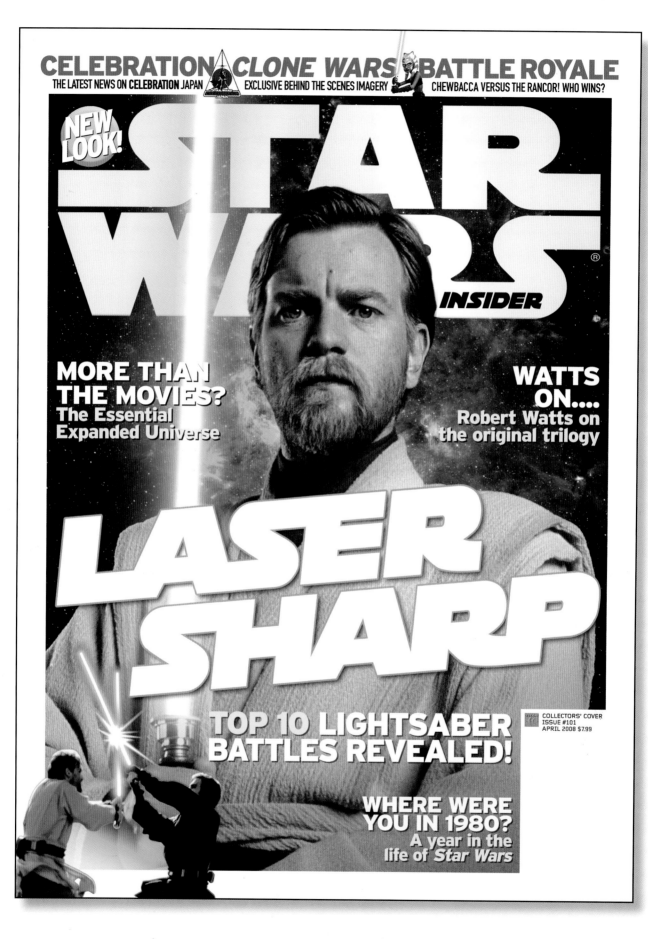

CELEBRATION CLONE WARS BATTLE ROYALE

THE LATEST NEWS ON **CELEBRATION** JAPAN | EXCLUSIVE BEHIND THE SCENES IMAGERY | CHEWBACCA VERSUS THE RANCOR! WHO WINS?

NEW LOOK!

STAR WARS
INSIDER
®

MORE THAN THE MOVIES?
The Essential Expanded Universe

WATTS ON....
Robert Watts on the original trilogy

LASER SHARP

COLLECTORS' COVER
ISSUE #101
APRIL 2008 $7.99

TOP 10 LIGHTSABER BATTLES REVEALED!

WHERE WERE YOU IN 1980?
A year in the life of *Star Wars*

"IF YOU STRIKE ME DOWN"
THE WEAPON OF A JEDI

ISSUE 101
MAY/JUNE 2008

Star Wars: The Last of the Jedi: Reckoning, a young reader's novel by Jude Watson, published by Scholastic (May)

Star Wars: Legacy of the Force: Invincible by Troy Denning released by Del Rey (May)

Star Wars Omnibus: Droids published by Dark Horse Comics (June)

Star Wars: Coruscant Nights I: Jedi Twilight by Michael Reaves, published by Del Rey (June)

There are many kinds of lightsaber fight in the *Star Wars* saga. In the order that audiences originally saw them, there's the first one: Obi-Wan confronts Darth Vader on the Death Star! There's the most emotionally charged one: Luke and Vader tear up Cloud City—and Luke's heart! There's the epic one: Who could forget the three-way battle between Darth Maul, Qui-Gon and Obi-Wan? And, of course, there's the fateful one on which the whole saga turns: Obi-Wan and Vader/Anakin dueling to the seeming death on Mustafar! They're all great, and all for wildly different reasons.

This top 10 list from 2008 is notable for the fact that it comes from an era when there were far fewer fights to choose from! Who would be included if we repeated the feature now? Rey vs. Kylo Ren? Anakin and Obi-Wan vs Asajj Ventress? I think I'd cast my vote for Kanan and Ezra's spirited fight against Darth Vader in *Star Wars Rebels*!

One thing is for sure, as long as there are Sith and Jedi in the galaxy, there will be plenty of lightsaber duels to come...—**Jonathan Wilkins**

THE GREATEST EVER...
LIGHTSABER BATTLES

FOR SOME PEOPLE THEY ARE WHAT *STAR WARS* IS ALL
ABOUT—THOSE MOMENTS WHEN THE LIGHTSABER BLADE
IS IGNITED AND BATTLE COMMENCES. BUT THEY'RE NOT
JUST ABOUT ACTION! THESE CONFRONTATIONS ARE OFTEN
THE MOST EMOTIONALLY CHARGED MOMENTS OF THE SAGA.
WORDS: PAUL SIMPSON

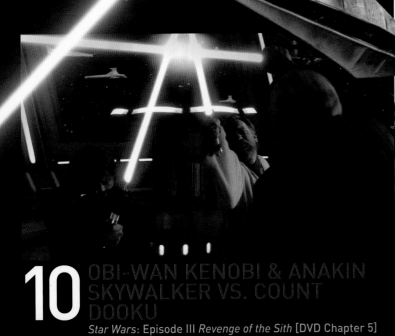

10 OBI-WAN KENOBI & ANAKIN SKYWALKER VS. COUNT DOOKU

Star Wars: Episode III *Revenge of the Sith* [DVD Chapter 5]

The first lightsaber battle of the final *Star Wars* movie is a rematch between the Jedi Master, his apprentice, and the Sith Lord; Dooku speaks for the whole audience when he says he's been looking forward to it. The action is fast and furious even before Dooku improves the odds by incapacitating Obi-Wan, but it steps up another notch when an angry Skywalker faces off against Dooku. When Anakin gives in to his hate, and maybe even the fear that Dooku senses, the Jedi takes the advantage. Anakin gets his revenge for losing his arm, cutting Dooku off at the wrists, before giving in to the dark side and obeying Palpatine's orders to kill the Count. The hatred in Anakin's eyes doesn't bode well for anyone who crosses his path in the future, and gets *Revenge of the Sith* off to a stunningly dramatic start.

9 OBI-WAN KENOBI VS. DARTH VADER

Star Wars: Episode IV *A New Hope* [DVD Chapter 38]

It's the lightsaber battle that has been re-enacted in schoolyards around the world for over 30 years, but it's on our list at number nine because, compared with the other lightsaber fights we see in the later installments of the *Star Wars* saga, it's a bit slow. There are still hints of Anakin's arrogance in Darth Vader's demeanor as he's convinced that defeating his old teacher is going to be easy. Despite his age, Kenobi is still spry, even if neither he nor Vader indulge in any of the acrobatics that characterized their battle a mere 19 years earlier. It's still incredibly powerful, and marks a key emotional moment in the saga as Obi-Wan surrenders himself to the Force.

7 QUI-GONN JINN & OBI-WAN KENOBI VS. DARTH MAUL

Star Wars: Episode I *The Phantom Menace* [DVD Chapter 39]

It's the first big lightsaber duel of the new trilogy, and it doesn't disappoint. The first time Qui-Gon Jinn faced off against Darth Maul, the Jedi Master looked hopelessly out of his depth, so it's no surprise that he's better prepared when he and Obi-Wan meet Maul in the hangar on Naboo. You expect it to be a walkover, so it's surprising when it's anything but! Maul harnesses the power of the dark side against his Jedi opponents; when they get separated, it gives him another advantage over and above his skills with his unique double-bladed lightsaber. When Qui-Gon is killed, Obi-Wan has to be equally vicious, leading to one of the *Star Wars* moments to treasure the most: the look of surprise on Maul's face as he realizes that Obi-Wan has used the Force to grab Qui-Gon's lightsaber to cut him in two!

8 OBI-WAN KENOBI VS. GENERAL GRIEVOUS

Star Wars: Episode III *Revenge of the Sith* [DVD Chapters 21 & 24]

"So uncivilized," Obi-Wan mutters after he's had to use a blaster to dispose of General Grievous. And it sums up their battle. This isn't a heroic contest between Jedi Knights and Sith Lords—it's a down and dirty, no holds barred, old-fashioned fight-to-the-death. After seeing Grievous in action in the *Clone Wars* micro-series, expectations were running high for this particular fight, and audiences weren't disappointed. However, it's fairly low on our list because a large part of it doesn't involve lightsabers at all: Kenobi disarms Grievous (literally!) and then loses his own lightsaber during their chase across the planet. It might not have the grace and epic quality of a duel between Jedi Masters, but there's a desperation about the fight that we've not seen before, but would again during *Revenge of the Sith*'s dark climax.

6 YODA VS. THE EMPEROR

Star Wars: Episode III *Revenge of the Sith* [DVD Chapter 39 onwards]

There are two big battles at the end of *Revenge of the Sith* that every fan was waiting for: Obi-Wan against Anakin, and Yoda versus the Emperor. We knew that all the combatants would survive their encounters, but what would happen when the ultimate Force masters met? It doesn't start well for the Jedi Master, and the Emperor may have a point when he accuses Yoda of arrogance and too much self-confidence. The two seem equally matched no matter the weapon: lightsabers, Force pushes, or Force lightning. The battles between Yoda and Dooku, and Palpatine and Mace Windu seem like warm-ups, as both employ every tactic used in those fights, yet still find themselves unable to take the upper hand. Cutting between this battle and Obi-Wan and Anakin's final duel makes Yoda's defeat seem even more powerful, and there's a definite air of unfinished business as Yoda makes his hasty retreat.

5 MACE WINDU VS. PALPATINE
Star Wars: Episode III *Revenge of the Sith*
[DVD Chapter 27]

Let's be honest here: as soon as Samuel L. Jackson was cast as Mace Windu, we all looked forward to seeing him in serious fighting mode. He had a bit of action on Geonosis, but it's at this key point in *Revenge of the Sith* that he comes into his own. Windu is up against an enemy he really doesn't understand or even recognize until it's far too late. Despite Palpatine's revelation that he's a Sith Lord, Windu doesn't give up. It's another fast and furious battle that ends with Windu disarming the treacherous Chancellor and apparently having him at his mercy. How much Palpatine is faking his weakness, hoping that Anakin will take the initiative and deal with Windu, we'll never know. But it certainly looks like Windu is going to deliver the ultimate sanction until Anakin takes the fateful step on his path to becoming Darth Vader and chooses to defend Palpatine.

4 LUKE SKYWALKER VS. DARTH VADER
Star Wars: Episode V *The Empire Strikes Back*
[DVD Chapters 42, 44, 46]

"I am your father." Darth Vader's revelation tends to overshadow the battle between father and son that precedes it, yet it's one of the strongest in the entire saga. This isn't an almost-civilized duel, like the fight between Ben Kenobi and Vader on the Death Star. Luke is no pushover, and is able to use the Force to a much greater extent than Vader anticipates. Vader has little option but to keep Luke at bay, using the dark side to throw objects at him. Yet Luke continues to survive, and the final phase of their lightsaber duel sees Vader at his most unrestrained, almost using his lightsaber as a broadsword, hacking at his son to force him backwards. In the end the only way to stop Luke from fighting is to cut his hand off and as the shocked youngster clings on, Vader reveals the truth—but doesn't anticipate Luke's decision to sacrifice himself rather than join him.

3 YODA VS. COUNT DOOKU
Star Wars: Episode II *Attack of the Clones* [DVD Chapter 46]

When word got out before Attack of the Clones opened that Yoda was going to be in a lightsaber duel, fans wondered aloud whether it would be the film's highlight or low point. After all, Christopher Lee's Count Dooku is up there in age for a human, and we'd never seen the wizened 800-plus year-old Jedi Master do much more than walk very slowly. The small figure who hobbles on his walking stick into the secret hangar on Geonosis seems almost pathetically frail as he adopts a stance preparing for battle. He may look a bit comic, but there's nothing funny about what follows. After all, it's Yoda who's been teaching Jedi apprentices for the past eight centuries! There are more parries and thrusts, jumps and attacks than in any of the previous fights. It's a battle between two masters of their art, lightsabers flashing so fast you can hardly follow it. Incredibly, the whole confrontation takes less than two and a half minutes, with only 45 seconds or so of lightsaber action!

2 LUKE SKYWALKER VS. DARTH VADER & THE EMPEROR
Star Wars: Episode VI *Return of the Jedi* [DVD Chapter 37 onwards]

It's the battle that the entire saga has been building towards, as the "*new hope*" of the Jedi confronts the ultimate evil in Emperor Palpatine—but which side will Darth Vader be on? The Emperor doesn't have any loyalty to Vader, no more than he did to Dooku, and whichever Skywalker wins, he will still have a pawn. He watches father and son battle with a raw passion as Luke fights to keep the evil of the Sith away from his sister Leia. Then when Vader's arm is chopped off, and Luke refuses the Emperor's "invitation" to join him, Palpatine turns on Luke. Only Vader can save his son. At most times, and particularly in his weakened state, Vader wouldn't have stood a chance against the power emanating from his Master, but the light side of the Force gives him the strength he needs. This is the only battle in the saga in which both opponents die: The Emperor's body explodes as it enters the reactor core, and Anakin Skywalker dies in his son's arms a few minutes later. Although Vader had claimed that the circle was complete when he encountered Ben Kenobi on the Death Star, it really was complete now, as the good side in Anakin finally helped return balance to the Force.

EXPANDED UNIVERSE >>

THE GREATEST EVER....
LIGHTSABER BATTLES

Lightsaber battles feature widely in the *Star Wars* Expanded Universe of novels, comic books, videogames, and animated adventures. Here's a few that *Insider* recommends you should check out:

Jedi: Mace Windu (comic book)
Sam Jackson's Mace Windu wields his purple-bladed lightsaber against a group of rogue Jedi.

Tales of the Jedi: The Sith War (comic book)
An epic, with a lot of double-bladed lightsaber action.

Legacy of the Force: Tempest (novel)
Luke Skywalker faces off against his first love in a knock-down, drag-out lightsaber fight.

Republic: "Show of Force." (comic book)
Mace Windu lights up his purple blade once again.

Jedi Knight: Dark Forces II (video game)
Kyle Katarn sometimes swaps his Bryar pistol for a lightsaber.

Darth Maul: Shadow Hunter (novel)
The moody Zabrak with the double-bladed lightsaber gets a back-story!

The New Jedi Order: Dark Tide (novels)
Features awesome lightsaber duels.

Clone Wars (animated micro-series)
Asajj Ventress is not only tested by her Master, Count Dooku (Chapter VII) but she also faces Anakin Skywalker in a rain-drenched super-duel in the jungles of Yavin 4 (Chapter XVIII).

1 OBI-WAN KENOBI VS. ANAKIN SKYWALKER

Star Wars: Episode III *Revenge of the Sith* [DVD Chapter 38 onwards]

For nearly 30 years we knew that the battle between Darth Vader and Ben Kenobi on board the Death Star was a rematch between the former Jedi Master and his apprentice. *Revenge of the Sith* finally provided us with the original, cataclysmic clash of the titans. While *Return of the Jedi* shows us Vader's redemption, and is the emotional climax of the saga, Episode III brought fans the big moment we'd all been waiting for. It came down to a massive lightsaber duel between two evenly matched opponents. The lightsabers flash furiously against the backdrop of volcanic Mustafar; while it's said that only a fool fights in a burning house, these two don't have an option. The planet erupts around them as neither will give ground. John Williams' magnificent score is operatic in scope as the two men duel back and forth, their lightsabers often the only items that aren't glowing orange or red on screen. It's epic, it dominates the movie—and fittingly, the final filmed battle of the saga is the finest. ☻

And Finally: Han vs the tauntaun!
Even in the movies, lightsabers can be put to novel uses. Our favorite is Han vs the tauntaun, in which the heroic Corellian waits until the creature freezes to death before daring to tackle it. We can only assume the awful smell he discovers is the tauntaun's revenge...

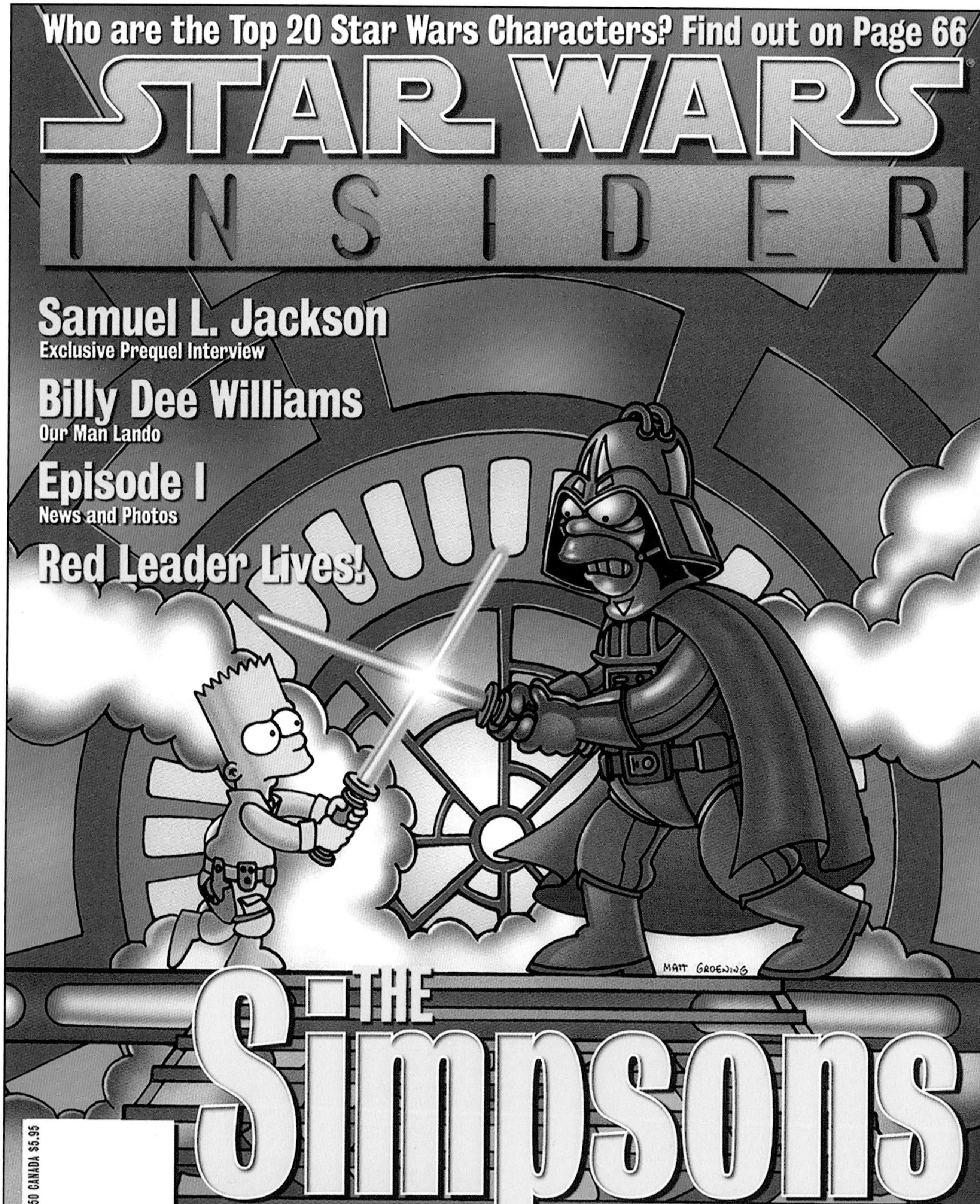

Who are the Top 20 Star Wars Characters? Find out on Page 66
STAR WARS
INSIDER
Samuel L. Jackson
Exclusive Prequel Interview
Billy Dee Williams
Our Man Lando
Episode I
News and Photos
Red Leader Lives!
MATT GROENING
THE Simpsons STRIKE BACK
STAR WARS ON TV'S MOST POPULAR ANIMATED SHOW
ISSUE 38 U.S.A $4.50 CANADA $5.95
The Simpsons TM and © 1998 Twentieth Century Fox Film Corporation. All Rights Reserved

SAMUEL L. JACKSON
MACE WINDU

ISSUE 38
JUNE/JULY 1998

*Star Wars: The Mandalorian Armor,
The Bounty Hunter Wars: Book 1*
by K. W. Jeter, published by
Bantam Spectra (June)

Star Wars: X-wing: Iron Fist
by Aaron Allston, published by
Bantam Spectra (July)

*Star Wars: The Essential Guide
to Planets and Moons*, by Daniel
Wallace with illustrations by
Brandon McKinney and Scott
Kolins, published by Del Rey
(July)

Dark Horse publishes
*Star Wars: Tales of the Jedi:
Redemption* Issue 1: "A Gathering
of Jedi," by Kevin J. Anderson and
artist Chris Gossett (July)

"I'll do anything to be in a *Star Wars* movie. I don't care! I'll even play a
stormtrooper!" It's the kind of thing any fan might have said when in earshot
of somebody that might be able to make such a dream come true. I can
remember when Samuel L. Jackson confessed his love of *Star Wars* and made
the plaintive plea above on the British TV show, *TFI Friday* during an interview
with Chris Evans (no, not his fellow Avenger!). Word got to George Lucas, and
he cast Jackson as Mace Windu—one of the most intriguing Jedi in the entire
saga. Such was Jackson's power that he even persuaded George Lucas that
Mace should carry a purple-bladed lightsaber, a complete departure from the
traditional color scheme.—**Jonathan Wilkins**

*Samuel Leroy Jackson (born December 21, 1948) achieved prominence and
critical acclaim in the early 1990s with films such as* Jungle Fever *(1991),*
Patriot Games *(1992), and* Jurassic Park *(1993). His collaborations with Quentin
Tarantino include* Pulp Fiction *(1994),* Jackie Brown *(1997), and* The Hateful
Eight *(2015). He also plays Nick Fury in the wildly popular Marvel Cinematic
Universe movies.*

PULP JEDI

an interview
with EPISODE I star

Samuel L. Jackson

BY SCOTT CHERNOFF

When Quentin Tarantino's landmark *Pulp Fiction* hit theaters in 1994, it was easy to think that Samuel L. Jackson—who played Jules, the eloquent hitman who has a spiritual epiphany—came out of nowhere. His performance was so electrifying, so engaging, so powerful, that most audiences emerged from the experience convinced they had seen a star born.

But the truth was that Samuel L. Jackson had been right in front of us for years, albeit with few opportunities to showcase his incredible talents. Indeed, before *Pulp Fiction*, Jackson had small roles in some of the best-loved movies of the '80s and '90s: *Goodfellas, Do the Right Thing, Ragtime, True Romance, Coming to America, Jurassic Park.* There was *Juice, Menace II Society, Sea of Love, School Daze,* and *Patriot*

Games (with Harrison Ford), and more plays than you can shake a stick at.

In 1991, the actor, a New York City native, finally started to gain wide attention with his extraordinary performance in Spike Lee's *Jungle Fever* (1991), which earned him a special award at France's Cannes Film Festival. His character, a crack addict named Gator Purify, veered from hilarious to frightening, but

Jackson also made him sadly human.

Yet it wasn't until *Pulp Fiction*—which afforded him one of his most interesting and complex characters, as well as an Academy Award-winning script chockfull of juicy, beguiling monologues—that Jackson had a chance to really show his stuff. Since then, Jackson has used his newfound stardom to successfully straddle the line between big-time Hollywood blockbusters and off-beat independent fare, and in the process he's become one of the biggest stars on the silver screen. »

Photo by Giles Keyte

>> Samuel L. Jackson (seen here in costume) plays a Jedi Master and a member of the Jedi Council in *Star Wars*: Episode I.

Since *Pulp Fiction*, Jackson has turned in diverse, compelling performances in *Fresh*, *Jackie Brown* (which re-teamed him with Tarantino), *187*, *A Time to Kill*, *Hard Eight*, *Tree's Lounge*, *Losing Isiah*, and *Die Hard: With a Vengeance*. He also produced 1997's most profitable American independent film, the acclaimed *Eve's Bayou*, in which he also starred.

You'd think that with a resumé like that, Jackson would hardly have to go asking for jobs. Yet that's just what the actor did, in interview after interview, to get his role in Episode I of the upcoming *Star Wars* prequel trilogy. In 1996, Jackson told the *Insider* he was an enormous fan of *Star Wars* and said, "I'm trying to find George Lucas now so I can be in his prequel." (Wouldn't you have done the same if you had his clout?)

So now that Samuel L. Jackson's dream has come true, the *Insider* returned to chat with the actor about the latest powerhouse entry in his filmography.

up the first day it was showing, got down to the theater. There was no line—just a bunch of heads out there, hanging out, waiting for the movie to start. We got in, everybody sat down, just waiting for it to happen, and it was everything we wanted it to be. I don't remember if I

Then it must have been quite a feeling to be welcomed into that universe for Episode I.

I was awed. It's pretty awesome to just show up on the set. It's something that you've always imagined. You're there, and all of the sudden, you're in it. **>>**

>> *Just an opportunity to go to the Ranch was cool for me. I rolled on up there, and we sat down and talked and had a great old time. George is cool.*

Did you really win your role in Episode I by announcing to the world that you were a huge *Star Wars* fan and would do anything to get a part in the new trilogy?

I guess so. You know, you do those interviews, and people always ask you that question, "Are there any directors that you haven't worked with that you want to work with?" I remembered George was making these movies, and I started to say George Lucas. I said it to the guy hosting this TV show in London when they were there in pre-production [on the prequel], and somebody got word to them.

Then when I was in Vallejo last year shooting *Sphere*, I got this call that said, "Well you're close by—you should go by the Ranch and visit George. He hears you're interested in the movies." And I go, "Yeah, no problem!" Just an opportunity to go to the Ranch was cool for me. I rolled on up there, and we sat down and talked, and had a great old time. George is cool.

Is it true you saw *Star Wars* the day it opened in 1977?

Well, I was waiting for it, because I had seen all these trailers at the theater, so I just got

sat through the next screening or what.

And you remained a big fan over the years?

Totally. I just kept keeping up with it.

What is it about *Star Wars* that you loved so much?

Well it was new, it was different. It was everything I had always wanted a film about space to be—you know, guys with lightsabers, really fast-moving planes, the costumes— everything was just right. It was like somebody had stepped into my mind and had taken everything that I wanted to happen and made it happen.

Having seen all those old pirate movies, all of a sudden, here were guys sword-fighting again, with lightsabers. I'm a huge Errol Flynn fan, and I watched all of *Commander Cody* and a bit of *Star Trek* and all those programs, but it wasn't the same for me. It was missing something, and George found all those things that were missing, and made it happen.

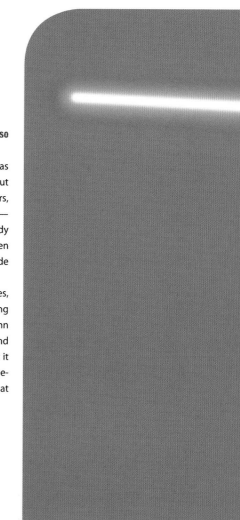

George only gave me the six pages I was in. It was just enough to pique my interest in what happened before and what's going to happen afterwards. I have no idea what the story is or what goes on. I'll be as in the dark as everybody else when I walk into the theater.

glad to be here—I'm not going to push it, I'm just gonna do my thing and stay cool.

Would you ever accept a part in a film without reading its entire script under non-*Star Wars* circumstances?

No, not at all. No way. But what do you expect? You expect a *Star Wars* movie, and you're gonna be part of it.

Do you know if you'll return for Episode II or III?

I don't know if *anybody* did a sequel deal. Of course, I don't know anything about any of

>> *It was everything I had wanted a film about space to be—you know, guys with lightsabers, really fast-moving planes, the costumes—everything was just right.*

Did the new stories excite you as much as the original film did?

I don't actually know that much about the movie. It's incredible. I have no idea what happened before I got there or what happened after I left. I was only there for four days, and

It's pretty bizarre having been a part of it and having people ask me questions about it and then going, "You know, I really don't know that much about it." They're always amazed—"Come on, he actually didn't let you read the script?" No, he didn't, and I didn't bother him about it. I'm just

that. I did this one, my character didn't die. There's a possibility of me coming back—cool.

Well, since your character hangs out with Jedi Master Yoda, I suppose there'd be a possibility of you coming back even if your character *did* die.

Even if I did, yeah!

What's it like working with Yoda?

It's like working with a great actor. He was there, totally involved, great facial expressions, great line reading, totally cool.

Does Frank Oz (the director/puppeteer who performs Yoda) disappear when you're working with Yoda?

Yeah, he's not there. He's there, but he's not there—Yoda's there, not Frank. It's pretty special the way it happens. It's great because all of a sudden they'll say *action* and Frank gets in there and Yoda kind of sits up and does all this stuff, and then when George says *cut*, Frank takes his hand out and it kind of slumps over. But the guys that are operating his ears and eyes still have their things on, so his ears are still moving and his eyes are going, and he's kind of slumped over like he's either hung over or not feeling well or something. It's like, "Man, somebody help Yoda!"

Being such a fan, was it difficult to calm down and focus on the work?

Not really. As soon as George says *action*, things just start to happen. You flow into the scene and try to give it all the reality you can give it, considering what's there—I actually met actors that I wouldn't know if they walked into my house today, because these guys were covered in make-up. There was one guy that I affectionately referred to as "Calimari," because that's what he kind of looked like. And there was another guy that looked like a giant lhasa apso, and there was a guy with a duck on his head—I don't know what that was. You try to ignore that—that's the norm. You just go ahead and do your thing.

Was your experience making *Star Wars* different from your memories of other big movies you've made like *Sphere* or *Jurassic Park*?

It actually had more of a low-budget feel to it than big-budget. There were none of the huge star trappings. There were no huge trailers around, I guess because we were in Britain, and there's a very different atmosphere around British sets. There's not the elaborate craft ser-

vice stuff going on. There's not a lot of P.A.s running around with their heads cut off—just kind of a calm that's there, the British way of stiff upper lip, no panic. It was totally laid-back there.

What was the toughest part of shooting Episode I for you?

The biggest thing for me was getting over the awe of being there, and making sure that I was doing something that was honest—not trying to pretend to be in a *Star Wars* movie, and trying to relax and just play naturally, and make it happen. George was satisfied, so I guess I did OK.

It's the kind of situation where you know you're keyed up in a certain kind of way because you're doing something that's interesting and exciting to you. You don't wanna overplay it because you think that it should be done a certain way, and I tried not to go in with any preconceived notion of what I was going to do and how I was going to do it. But I don't know if I achieved that. It's a strange sort of feeling for me, because I'm always pretty sure of what I'm doing.

>> ***... there was another guy that looked like a giant lhasa apso, and there was a guy with a duck on his head—I don't know what that was.***

How long did you have with the script to prepare before you were shooting?

Oh, I got it the day I showed up. It's not like

>> It's the kind of situation where you know you're keyed up in a certain kind of way because you're doing something that's interesting and exciting to you.

they were going to send me the pages early just in case I changed my mind and I'm gonna publish them.

So you didn't even know who your character was until you showed up?

Exactly.

How much time do you normally spend preparing for a role?

Usually, you have months, or at least some weeks before you have to do it. So this was unusual. It definitely added an intensity and a focus to it. Hey, he didn't hire me because I couldn't do it, I guess. He had enough faith in the fact that I could get it, come in, and be ready to go.

Did they give you any information or back-story for your character once you were there?

Nope. *[Laughs.]* Nope. None whatsoever.

Did you give yourself a back-story?

I didn't have time to go through it that much. I dealt with what I was doing and started to think a little bit about how he got to be in that place that he was in, why he was there, why he was that close to Yoda, or why *they* had

so many conversations and not him and other people. And I came up with some relevant facts that would relate to the stories that I did know, the things that came after and the kind of people that they are.

So you drew on the other *Star Wars* movies for inspiration?

Oh, of course.

Did your experience as producer of *Eve's Bayou* give you any insight into how full George Lucas' plate was during shooting?

Not necessarily. George is a whole different kind of entity in that he's writing it, he had the concept, he's directing it, he's going to work with the editor—George is a fabulous editor. He has a whole other kind of insight into the process than I have. I was just kind of there [on *Eve's Bayou*] overseeing and learning the job, learning how to read a budget sheet and figure out the things that I needed to do to make the next day work or keep the crew happy. So much goes on in being a producer.

Will you do it again?

Oh yeah, I'm definitely doing it again. I've got a couple projects that are in development,

and hopefully one will be ready to go by the end of the year.

Do you have any favorite movies you've done—or are they all your favorites?

No, no, they're not all my favorites! I actually really like all the action films. I had a great time doing *Die Hard*. I had a fabulous time doing *Long Kiss Goodnight*. I'm really proud of *Fresh* and *187*, and when I think of *Pulp Fiction* and *Jackie Brown*, those are great times. Quentin is such a fun filmmaker, his sets are great places to be.

What's the difference between a Quentin Tarantino set and a George Lucas set?

It's hard for me to say because I was only on George's set for four days, and I enjoyed it in a different kind of way because it's awesome just to sit there and look around and see who you're around and what's going on and know that you're a part of this very special thing. Plus you're also wondering, "I wonder what the rest of this set's going to look like when they finish putting the rest of the images in it."

But a Quentin set is like going to high school and being with all your best friends all day long, and there are no teachers around to tell you what to do and what not to do. So you end up laughing and doing the stuff that you

street theater, and then I started doing children's theater and repertory theater at this other company, I realized that I could make a living doing it, and I could have a great time. That made me kind of serious about it.

All of a sudden everything else became insignificant, and I threw myself into it. When I got up in the morning, I was at the theater in the drama department and I was building sets all day, and I would go and do this other job at the children's theater and then I had to come back to the theater at the school, and after that we had our own guerrilla street theater that we used to rehearse until 3 in the morning. It was an ongoing thing. It totally became part of my fabric, being an actor.

Do you still get the same buzz out of it?

Oh yeah, totally. If I didn't, I wouldn't do it. Folks are always saying, "Don't you want to direct?" I don't have that feeling. I have a burning desire to act, and I do. I don't think directing is a natural offshoot of what we do. I don't feel the need to exercise that kind of power over it yet. Plus I like my downtime in my trailer.

So was working with George Lucas everything you'd hoped it would be?

Oh, George is totally cool. He knows how he wants it to happen. He hired us, he trusted us, so he's not giving us a lot of direction. He's very low-key on set. He's the first director I've ever known to have airplanes flying over and

>> *A Quentin set is like going to high school and being with all your best friends all day long, and there are no teachers around to tell you what you do and what not to do.*

want to do. But if they give you an assignment, you find a fun way to get it done, and it still gets done. You're able to have more fun because you got it done quicker. That's a Quentin set.

Have you been an actor all your life?

I got into it because I was taking a speech class in college, and the guy offered us extra credit for the class if we'd do his play. I had never even been in the drama department, let alone gone to see a play on campus. After that I never stopped doing it.

What hooked you?

Sex, drugs, and—no [laughs]. I don't know, I just enjoyed the feeling of being up there on stage and making believe and not being myself and just having a great time. And that was it for a while. When I started to do

stuff falling around behind him and not yell *cut*. He'd just go, "Yeah, that was good for me." He has to do so much in post, that's the last thing he's worried about.

There was no tension, no pressure. People would have you believe that something that has that much secrecy around it would be a lot more tense or uptight, but it's not. I just hope this movie hits everybody the way it did the first time. It's the first part of a new trilogy, and I hope I'll be around for the rest! ☺

STAR WARS

INSIDER

REBEL ROUSER!

THE MAN BEHIND THE *STAR WARS* NEWSPAPER STRIPS!

FATE OF A JEDI?

PLUS!

DAWN OF THE JEDI
LEGO *STAR WARS*
BOBA FETT

SUPERVISING DIRECTOR DAVE FILONI ON AHSOKA, SEASON FIVE, AND MORE!

TITAN

ISSUE 140

U.S. $7.99
CAN $9.99

APRIL 2013

DAVE FILONI
STAR WARS: THE CLONE WARS

ISSUE 140
APRIL 2013

Vader's Little Princess by Jeffrey Brown, published by Chronicle Books

Fantasy Flight Games publish *The Search for Skywalker,* an expansion pack for *Star Wars: The Card Game*

LucasArts closes for business

Some interviews seem to come at the right moment. *Insider*'s interview with Dave Filoni, which I conducted as the fifth season of *The Clone Wars* was reaching its conclusion, was one such conversation.

As it turned out, this would be the last full season of *The Clone Wars*, which was soon to make way for *Star Wars Rebels*.

There was much to discuss, not least the emotionally shattering season finale, and Dave's honest, if often necessarily evasive style is in full effect here. There is an old showbusiness adage: always leave them wanting more. *The Clone Wars* certainly did that, and so does Dave Filoni!—**Jonathan Wilkins**

Dave Filoni (born June 7, 1974) is best known for his work on Avatar: The Last Airbender *and* Star Wars: The Clone Wars. *He is executive producer and supervising director on* Star Wars Rebels.

DAVE FILONI, SUPERVISING DIRECTOR OF *STAR WARS: THE CLONE WARS* ON SEASON FIVE, AHSOKA, BARRISS OFFEE, AND WHY HE LOVES THE PASSION OF THE FANS. INTERVIEW BY JONATHAN WILKINS.

UNEXPECTED JOURNEYS

"When I first started on *The Clone Wars*, I didn't know how long I'd be working for Lucasfilm—I just wanted to make the best show possible. I thought I'd be here maybe two years."—Dave Filoni (approaching his 8th year as supervising director on *Star Wars: The Clone Wars*).

It has always been a joy to talk with Dave Filoni. As any fan who has enjoyed his numerous convention appearances will tell you, he lives, breathes, and speaks *Star Wars*. Interviewing him for *Insider* is always one of the highlights of the job—usually a call from the London office to his Lucasfilm office at Big Rock Ranch in Marin County, California.

Here's a secret. This interview was done on Tuesday, January 16, some two months before we hit newsstands—and way before the finale of season five of *The Clone Wars* has been publically seen. *The Clone Wars'* ever-helpful PR representative, Tracy Cannobbio, lets Dave know the relevant dates; then, between the three of us, we decided that we could talk about the Alderaan-shattering climax to season five. If you didn't pay heed to the spoiler warning at the start of this interview, then know that we'll be giving a lot away. You have been warned!

THE DIVERSITY OF *STAR WARS*

We start by discussing the many challenges the show presents Filoni and his team. In the past, there have been technical barriers to break through: water, fire, and cloth simulation, for example. Happily the team has vanquished them, with insurmountable problems in the early seasons now solved. Filoni admits the challenges are less technical now, and more story-driven.

"We typically have about 22 episodes per season, and we have to try to decide what's going to make it out there or not. I know that some fans sometimes think they'd be happy with an entire season about Darth Maul, but we have such a wide-ranging fan base. We have stories for every type of fan.

"There's always the choice as to which characters are going to make it onto the screen. Sometimes we say, 'Wow, we didn't see this character all season long!' You can get so caught up telling these other stories that you don't even realize it. That's probably one of the biggest challenges: you have to juggle the characters and make sure you follow through with the characters' arcs."

Nothing is off-limits for the show's writers. "We just act like that. I don't know how relatively true it is. I don't tell the writers, 'Let's not do that.' It's more, 'Let's get this story right. Let's worry about that first.' We don't live by the restrictions we had five years ago.

"We always have to keep an eye on the budget. At certain points, it will push back and that's where we have to make a wide range of decisions—from *maybe Dooku's not wearing his cloak in this scene* to *how can we re-purpose these sets?* It's really the same issue that you would have on any movie, the same situations, the same problems. But I've never chosen to let the budget dictate the stories we're telling. The whole team wants this show to look good no matter what, and everybody just goes above and beyond while trying to reach that goal. I'm a considerably better director today for all of George's teaching than I was when I got here."

Above: Ahsoka, Huyang and the Younglings.

Right: The two sides of *Star Wars:* Darth Maul and Gunji represent the darker and more whimsical episodes of the show.

> ## "I'VE NEVER CHOSEN TO LET THE BUDGET DICTATE THE STORIES WE'RE TELLING. THE WHOLE TEAM WANTS THE SHOW TO LOOK GOOD."

Right, from top: Young Ganodi pilots an ancient Jedi cruiser with encouragement from Huyang; the Droid story arc provided much needed levity; Yoda in the legendary temple of Ilum.

SITH LORDS AND YOUNGLINGS

Season five's diverse stories have featured vengeful Sith Lords, droids on a mission, and themes of rebellion and sacrifice. Perhaps the most popular was the enchanting "younglings" episodes which featured some of the series' best aesthetics to date. Filoni, too, is a fan of that four-part arc. "I think that whole thing came out really well. Maybe it's just a little easier to relate it to the Original Trilogy, because you've got a band of young people who are coming together to overcome insurmountable odds—that's a pretty good theme in *Star Wars*! It brought some of the magic back, like showing how the Jedi make a lightsaber. That sort of thing we'd seen in the *Clone Wars* micro-series, but not really *per se* how George Lucas has envisioned it. He wanted to start the kids off much younger; it was more about Yoda's lesson, which I think really works to our advantage and to the story's advantage."

Was there any trepidation about centering an arc on the younglings when the show had grown in its maturity? "All the writers would tell you that in these meetings when George said, 'I want to do a series of stories about young Jedi,' it could go either way. It could be really good, or a groaner. The first thing discussed was how old these kids are going to be. I started drawing them immediately to get a visual idea of how it might look.

"When we were trying to work out which species to do, I did a little Kel Dorian kid [the same species as Plo Koon, Filoni's favorite character] who George immediately nixed. He said, 'No way! Too ugly!'

"Then it just kind of gained momentum in our imaginations, having the little Wookiee, Gunji, and deciding what they would look like. I did some research to figure out what the crystal caves would look like, too, to give it a sense of history. I put nice little clues in there for people playing The Old Republic to see some connectivity between the game and the history we've created. You can see their fleet symbol on the *Crucible* ship. Of course, there was also Huyang, voiced by David Tennant, who brought a great level of magic to his role and the story."

A NEW VOICE FOR THE REPUBLIC?

The show lost one of its finest actors last year when Ian Abercrombie, who played Palpatine, passed away. His replacement, Tim Curry, brings all-new facets to the character. "It was a very long search to find someone to replace Ian," Filoni reveals. "There are people who think they can do the voice, but it's different when you're reciting lines from the film; it's really about the magic of the acting and bringing the characters to life by saying things they've never said.

"What Tim really brings is a great level of experience, but also a kind of gravelly edge. He brings a nice level of sinister evil, something that he did all the way back in *Legend* [1985]. Ian's Darth Sidious voice was deep, but wasn't quite as gravelly as what Tim is doing," Filoni continues. "It's an interesting nuance and quite a shift in some ways.

I wish that Ian Abercrombie could have finished all of season five, but Tim is in one episode at the end of the season, along with a brief line that we inserted overlapping with Ian in 'Revival,' one of the Darth Maul episodes. I think it's the final line of the episode. Most people don't even notice the difference. It's a great hand-off in a way, to have someone like Tim Curry come in and portray this character now, and he does a really brilliant job."

Unless things get light and fluffy toward the end (Filoni assures me they won't), Season Five is the darkest season yet. A move from Friday nights to Saturday mornings might make you think that *The Clone Wars* would dial down the darker aspects of the show. Not so, says Filoni. "The Season Five episodes were already done before the time change. I would be more sensitive to it now, and say, 'Let's pull back on that a little bit.' I trust a network like Cartoon Network when they say when they want to show it. They are very experienced at doing that and I have more experience doing *Star Wars*. The ratings have really shown it was the right choice.

"But I think people are aware of how intense the show can get—and things are not going to get fluffier with Darth Maul around, that's for sure! Saturday mornings have never been this exciting!"

> "IT WAS A LONG SEARCH TO FIND SOMEBODY TO REPLACE IAN ABERCROMBIE AS PALPATINE. TIM CURRY HAS A GREAT LEVEL OF EXPERIENCE, BUT ALSO A GRAVELLY EDGE."

JEDI NO MORE?

Ahsoka's journey took an unexpected twist in the finale. While Filoni is clear that it's not the culmination of where the character is going, and there is more to come, he's sure it's going to get fans talking. As he lays out what's to come, more than one plot-point elicits an audible gasp from the writer of this article.

"This is a big year for Ahsoka and I'm very happy about how it went," says Filoni. "We knew we wanted to do a big arc with her to end this season. George is really onboard with her character, and I think he's really happy with how she's developed. We wanted to challenge her, so the opening sequence in the first part of the arc shows her flying toward Cato Neimoidia and the action is all about showing her in her prime, and how she is now capable. Anakin shouldn't have to worry about her, because she's the one that saves him. She has a bit of an edge to her, not unlike Anakin.

"As we move on, we challenge several things—one of which is something I've been feeding into the story for a long time, which is the people's perception of the Jedi and the Jedi Order. We find out in this arc that there are people protesting the war from within the Republic. There are people that blame the Jedi for the war and want them to stop.

"Ahsoka's journey, which involves a terrorist attack on the Jedi Temple, and Ahsoka being implicated for it, results in a big test of faith. It's a big eye-opener for her. She asks, 'Why isn't the Jedi Council rushing to my aid? Why aren't they defending me without question?' The real thing that you see is that the Jedi Council is pretty compromised because they have to play a political game. They know that if they defend Ahsoka, then it'll look like they're playing inside politics; it will fuel public dissension against the Jedi if they do not have her tried outside the Order. It's a test of her faith in the Jedi and her friends. That's what's at the heart of it."

As Filoni goes deeper into the story, he warns that my head will explode if he and the team have done their jobs right. Undeterred by the thought of working as a headless writer from then on, I compel him to continue. He tells the story of how Barriss Offee, the kindly and kind-of cute Jedi Padawan who befriended Ahsoka (we met her in the Geonosis arc back in Season Two), is a traitor! As Filoni admits, "I keep trying to sympathize with the readers who are going to pick up this issue of *Insider*, because they're going to want to

know: 'Dave, why did you do what you did in this arc?'

"The reason that Barriss is the head conspirator with these people that have been protesting the Jedi Order is because she believes the Order is corrupt, and are following a corrupt senate. She thinks they have lost their way and that the only thing the Council reacts to or believes in anymore is violence. And she's right, everything she says is true, but her reaction to the situation is wrong and it's devastating to Ahsoka. That is the main motivator at the end of this season for why Ahsoka does not come back to the Jedi Order. It's a combination of her faith being shaken and the way the Jedi Council operates, because she can't deny what Barriss says is true.

"This has huge repercussions. We are foreshadowing everything in the final arc of this season. It foreshadows the Empire, because we see Tarkin's military institution really rising up in a way that hasn't been seen before. We see the massive Republic courtroom and it completely reflects the Death Star in every possible way. There's the feeling that the Jedi are uncomfortable in it. You really see the teeth of the machine that's going to destroy them."

CHALLENGING THE FANS

As with any drama, each plot goes through many changes before transmission. "There was a moment when we were talking with George about the finale, about how the Council tries to bring Ahsoka back to the Order," Filoni explains. "They describe the whole ordeal at the end of this season as her great trial and that she's a better Jedi than she would've been otherwise for this tragedy. The original intention was just to bring her back, but then the writers and I thought about how she'd react to this—and decided that she should turn them down. It works on many levels, not least of which is that Ahsoka is a teenager and how often do teenagers react to authority when authority is wrong or authority wrongs them? I'm hoping it's unexpected, and there are a couple of things there for me to get letters about. If we're not challenging fans with characters and their relationships, then we end up being predictable."

Ahsoka's fate may hang in the balance at the close of this season, but Filoni admits that, for the first time, her ultimate fate has been decided. "George and I sat down and ironed out the end of it. We actually know what happens to Ahsoka and the other characters. There are several episodes planned with her and what happens to her from this point."

Of course, key to Ahsoka's popularity is the performance of Ashley Eckstein, for whom Filoni is full of praise, enthusing about a trailer that Lucasfilm is putting together to promote the arc. "She's spectacular—the best she's ever been! It's a wonderful piece of acting by Ashley. But, at the same time, it's so her! She came to us not knowing much about *Star Wars*. I had this actor who was going to play a very important role in this series and didn't know how important the role was going to be. Her real life involvement in the show has really mirrored the character's evolution.

"When we recorded the final scene between Ahsoka and Anakin this season, I sent all the other actors away. I said, 'Everybody go, except for you two.' We recorded the scene with them, and then George and I watched it. George wanted to make some changes—nuances to the dialogue—and I had to bring them back in, and then we changed it again, which ensured nobody knew what the actual ending was going to be! We just continued to work on that final moment. I think for Ashley and Matt

it was especially moving. I do terrible things to her—I told her that I wasn't going to see her for a while because she was out of the storyline for a bit and she got quite sad. Whether it's true or not doesn't matter—I'm the director and I need to motivate her!

"Ashley and Matt give powerful performances these episodes and I think they've really grown to love those characters. It worked really well.

"Our composer, Kevin Kiner, watched all four episodes with me and we pinpointed where we really wanted to hit with the music—we don't do that for every episode," Filoni continues. "Joel Aron's lighting was amazing—one of the skies you see in the final scene between Ahsoka and Anakin outside the Jedi Temple was actually inspired by one of the trips I take to L.A. to do the voice recordings. We were driving back from the airport. I looked at the sky and it had just rained. I thought, *This sky is perfect*! It's one of those times that all the new technology we have at our fingertips to take pictures really came in handy. I took a bunch of pictures of the sky and gave them to Joel. Everything kind of fell into place—I think they're some of the best-rendered episodes we've ever done."

Clockwise, from top: Gregor, a Republic Commando; Obi-Wan Kenobi in Mandalorian armor; Adi Gallia takes on Savage Oppress; Ahsoka faces trial; A Mandalorian Super Commando.

> "THERE'S ONE CHARACTER IN PARTICULAR THAT GOES DOWN AND I THOUGHT, *I KNOW SOMEBODY WHO IS A BIG FAN. MAYBE WE SHOULD SEND A SYMPATHY LETTER!*"

CLEANING HOUSE

The season also saw numerous characters killed off. Filoni jokes that, "We're cleaning house!" *Star Wars* fans are always vocal about favorite characters being written out—just look at the reaction to Boba Fett being killed off in *Return of the Jedi*. Is Filoni ready to face the more vocal fans?

"It just shows that they care," he responds. "I don't mind it at all. I think it's a good thing. If we weren't getting any reaction, it would stink. There's one character in particular that goes down and I thought, *I know someone who's a big fan of that character. Maybe we should have the whole crew sign a sympathy letter and send it over in the mail.*"

The season also saw the return of the Mandalorians—characters who have not been without controversy in the past. Filoni reflects on their inclusion and the way that they have differed from the depictions in the novels.

"I think at the end of the day, what's been developed on the show with George feels like it fits more with the bigger mythology that he was making: that they are a capable warrior race and that their culture changes and develops over the years and is not always this one-dimensional thing. I think this view of it gives them a more interesting history. That's one of our strengths as a franchise—just like with our episode arcs, you can be a fan of any number of episodes and you can be a fan of any era of *Star Wars* or not. Before, you'd hear fans saying, 'I love the originals!' or 'I don't like the prequels!' but now there's a very vocal group that love the prequels and are tired of hearing older fans say how much they like the originals! Now there is a middle group, raised on this cartoon and that's their *Star Wars*! Then behind them is going to be fans who like the new upcoming trilogy!

"Imagine fast-forwarding 15 years from now to that year's *Star Wars* Celebration, and imagine what the demographic is going to be like. It's going to be amazing."

A CENTURY OF CLONES

For a man who thought he'd be working on the show for two years, Filoni hit a major milestone in January with 100 episodes of the show. "To give George credit, he always talked in terms of 100 episodes or more," Filoni reflects. "I thought, *Wow, that's a lot*, right back when we were still figuring out how to make starfighters fly properly. We sailed past that. Then I blinked and we passed 100 episodes. But we need 100 more just to finish what we're trying to do!"

The show has introduced a staggering number of characters who have struck a chord with fans. Some feel like they've been a part of *Star Wars* mythology since the start. Aside from Ahsoka Tano, the roll-call of fan favorites is extraordinary, with Cad Bane, Embo, Captain Rex, and Hondo amongst many standing alongside the movie greats. Filoni's contribution to the saga is met with a modest response: "When I step back and look at it, I almost feel like I didn't have anything to do with it because it's *Star Wars*. I have such respect for *Star Wars*. When I see a fan wearing a T-shirt with Rex on it, a *Clone Wars* backpack, or they're dressed up like Ahsoka, it just blows my mind. I always want to just take time out to talk to them because it's something we had direct involvement in. I know all the people behind it, from the people who paint the characters to the ones who model the helmets, to the ones who did the design.

"I don't feel the ownership over it because I still feel so privileged to be a part of it. It's still a real responsibility and I don't take for granted that I can just put things into play in the *Star Wars* universe. I try to do things that I know the fans, George, and *Star Wars* needs and can use, not something that I want to put in there just because I can. It's incredible—just to be a part of it.

"I have a wall at work that's completely dedicated to fans in costumes from *The Clone Wars* specifically, just so my crew can walk past it and see how much care and attention to detail the fans put in when paying tribute to our work. It's incredibly flattering. From the first time hearing George talking about Ahsoka as one of his own—because he did create her—her genesis was really through sketching out the character. Henry Gilroy and I wanted to have a Padawan character, so seeing her as an action figure and seeing the pride that George has in the character is just tremendous."

> "TO GIVE GEORGE LUCAS CREDIT, HE ALWAYS TALKED IN TERMS OF 100 EPISODES OR MORE. I THOUGHT, *WOW, THAT'S A LOT....*"

Left: Captain Rex swiftly became a fan favorite.

Right: Goodbye Ahsoka? While the season ends on a cliffhanger, Filoni promises more to come.

Top, from left: Hondo, another much-loved character; Darth Maul battles Pre Vizsla in a breathtaking fight sequence.

LEGACY

The cast and crew of the original trilogy are still much in demand for interviews and convention appearances 35 years on from the original film. It's interesting to consider what *The Clone Wars* legacy will be. Filoni is optimistic. "I keep telling the crew that we don't know what effect we've had yet, because fans don't lose momentum with *Star Wars* as they get older; they seem to gain it! I can see a time in 10 years when *Clone Wars* era fans are older and have money to spend on collectibles. They'll want their incredibly detailed Ahsoka statues and Captain Rex accurate blasters and all that stuff.

"I love it when people take them over into the live-action world—I think that's just great. The day I went to Walt Disney World for *Star Wars* Weekends and (one of the girls dressed as) Ahsoka Tano walked up and started talking to me, I was like 'Okay, wow—that's weird but awesome!'

"It's been an amazing experience and still is. I couldn't ask for a better situation or a better group of people to work with, especially with Kathleen Kennedy now taking charge. It's just another level of development and I get to see things in a different way now. I've had some exciting days here, even just this week—if you could only know, but you can't!"

But surely sometimes, it can be tough to get criticized? Filoni is pragmatic. "I think when you're a creator, working on something like *Star Wars* or anything that has a fan base, you have to accept the discussions, the arguments, even some of the hatred, comes from a place of passion and sometimes wanting to be a part of it. Most fans just want to be heard and I hope through some of the things they've seen on the show or experienced or when they get to talk to me or Joel or any of the cast, that they feel like they're always heard and that we really appreciate the time they take and the interest they have and what they have to say."

And so the interview draws to a close. Aside from the usual pleasantries and joking that Filoni will be the only attendee at Celebration Europe II (at the time of the interview he was the only guest to be announced) with a convention full of angry Barriss Offee fans, it's time for him to return—to what could well be the best job in the world.

EXPANDED

Read Dave's blog at starwarsblog.starwars.com

UNIVERSE

BATTLE READY!
STAR WARS: THE CLONE WARS EPISODE GUIDE

FIGHT!
LANDO TAKES ON HAN

CARRIE FISHER!
ON HAN SOLO, HER HAIRSTYLES, AND HOLLYWOOD

STAR WARS

INSIDER

JEDI MASTER

EXCLUSIVE INTERVIEW WITH YODA VOICE ACTOR TOM KANE

ISSUE #110
AUG 2009 £3.99

WICKET'S WORLD!
Warwick Davis
Talks Furballs!

BLASTER!
Books, Incoming, Toys,
Classic Scene, Ask Lobot,
Retro, Bounty Hunters,
Bantha Tracks and More!

TOM KANE
YODA

ISSUE 110
AUGUST 2009

Star Wars: Fate of the Jedi: Omen by Christie Golden, published by Del Rey

Ladybird Books publish adaptations of *The Clone Wars* episodes *"Downfall of a Droid"* and *"Destroy Malevolence"*

Star Wars Legacy: Tatooine, Part 1 (issue 37) published by Dark Horse Comics. Written by John Ostrander and Jan Duursema

"Ambush", the first transmitted episode of *Star Wars: The Clone Wars*, is a showcase for Yoda as he defeats Separatist forces on Toydaria. It's a fun, action-packed episode and, in a scene where Yoda motivates the clones, incredibly warm. A vast part of that comes from Tom Kane's delightful performance as Yoda. There could have been no better way to set the tone for the show to come.—**Jonathan Wilkins**

Tom Kane (born April 15, 1962) has provided voices for numerous TV shows and videogames, including Wolverine and the X-Men, *Marvel vs Capcom 3: Fate of Two Worlds,* Next Avengers: Heroes of Tomorrow, The Avengers: Earth's Mightiest Heroes, Foster's Home for Imaginary Friends, Kim Possible, The Powerpuff Girls, The Angry Beavers, *and* The Wild Thornberrys. *He also played the Chancellor in Tim Burton's animated movie* 9 *(2009), and was the announcer at the 78th, 80th, 83rd, and 84th Academy Awards.*

TOM KANE—MASTER OF ANIMATED VOICES FOR *STAR WARS* AND BEYOND—COMMANDS THE CLONE WARS AS THE VOICE OF JEDI MASTER YODA. WORDS: SCOTT CHERNOFF

VOICE OF THE FORCE

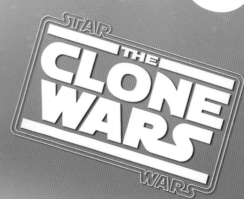

Yoda—the ultimate Jedi Master, a character known and loved throughout the world, whose voice was created by one of the most legendary puppeteers and voice actors of all time. You'd think that taking over the character from Frank Oz would be such a daunting and difficult assignment that it would be all one performer could handle.

But not when that performer is Tom Kane, one of the top voice-over artists working today, and the man who has given voice to some of the most memorable and iconic animated characters of the last dozen years. In fact, Yoda is merely the most prominent of a seemingly endless stream of *Star Wars* roles Kane continues to tackle. A born mimic, Kane even admitted he dedicated no time to preparing for the powerful role—other than the

years he'd spent as a devoted *Star Wars* fan.

"The Yoda thing just kind of happened," Kane tells *Star Wars Insider*, explaining that he was already in a recording studio playing another character for a LucasArts video game. "I'm a *Star Wars* nerd," he says, "so I would sit there looking through the script, and I would try to do my best Grand Moff Tarkin or Boba Fett or whoever. I was goofing around one day, and saw some Yoda lines, so of course I was trying to do my very best Yoda, and the producer looked up and said, 'Can you do that again?'

"What I didn't know," he continues, "was that Frank Oz was very busy at that point because he had become a very successful director. So they played my Yoda for George Lucas and got approval, and suddenly I found myself doing Yoda for videogames, and that led to toys and commercials. When it came time to do *Star Wars: The Clone Wars*, somebody up north said, 'We're just going to use Tom.'"

CAST OF CHARACTERS
By that point, of course, George Lucas and his team had good reason to be confident in Kane's formidable abilities. He'd already played Yoda in several LucasArts games, such as Jedi Power Battles, *Star Wars*: Galactic Battlegrounds, Super Bombad Racing, Jedi Starfighter, *Star Wars*: Battlefront I and II, and the videogame adaptation of *Revenge of the Sith*, among many others. Most memorably of all,

Kane voiced the sage Jedi Master in the *Clone Wars* micro-series that ran on Cartoon Network from 2003 to 2005.

Kane's Yoda voice—confident, resonant, and true to Oz's original vision—is the culmination of a saga that began with Kane's work on the early LucasArts title, The Dig. That success led to Kane's entry into the *Star Wars* universe, where he has provided voices for nearly every videogame the company has ever created. Kane started out playing random stormtroopers and Imperial officers before going on to tackle more familiar characters like Lobot, Admiral Ackbar, C-3PO, Nien Nunb, Bib Fortuna, and even those three characters he used to impersonate during his goof-off breaks: Boba Fett, Grand Moff Tarkin, and Yoda.

Indeed, it was Kane's success in the videogame world that led to the next step, about which he'd always dreamed: animation. That dream has come true many times over, with Kane having voiced unforgettable characters like Professor Utonium and the villainous Him on *The Powerpuff Girls*, Darwin the chimpanzee of *The Wild Thornberrys*, Mr. Herriman on *Foster's Home for Imaginary Friends*, Lord Monkey Fist of *Kim Possible*, and Magneto on *Wolverine and the X-Men*. He also lent his many voices to such 'toons as *Duck Dodgers*, *Shrek the Third*, and late 1990s animated series starring Spider-Man, Iron Man, and the Incredible Hulk—not to mention his continued videogame voice work, which has included Gandalf for The Lord of the Rings: The Fellowship of the Ring and

Commissioner Gordon in the Batman game, Arkham Asylum.

PHONING IT IN!

Yet the scope of Kane's work is so wide that all of those famous characters are just a small slice of it.

In fact, if you've turned on your TV or radio today, chances are you've already heard him. Kane works every day—which is virtually unheard of among voice performers—and the vast majority of his work is as an announcer, voicing everything from promotional spots for TV crime dramas to the trailers for *Monsters vs. Aliens*. He's been the official voice of the Academy Awards a few times, and he's done so many commercials and movie trailers, he's lost count. On the day *Star Wars Insider* caught up with him, Kane was between recording sessions, one as an announcer for CBS promos and the other for a character on Adult Swim's *The Boondocks*.

He does it nearly all from a home studio in Kansas City, his hometown that he returned to in 2005 with his wife and six children after 20 years in Los Angeles. Kane is now so in-demand that he can literally "phone it in," recording his voice over a high-bandwidth ISDN line

that connects him to the Los Angeles studios where the directors sit.

"I grew up here, and my wife and I met at the University of Kansas," Kane says. "Our families are here on both sides, and we wanted to let the kids get to know their grandparents."

Growing up just outside of Kansas City, where he was born in 1962, Kane never expected to be working on major Hollywood projects, but he did have a talent for mimicry and voices from an early age, a skill he started to develop in the local media.

"My mom tells me that when I was three years of age, my grandfather would be watching the football game and cussing at the television in German, and I would just repeat what Grandpa said. He would laugh and say, 'Ya, the kid's got a pretty good German accent.' I used to embarrass the heck out of my sister in the grocery store, because we'd be in the cereal aisle and I'd go, 'Frosted Flakes, they're grrrrrrreat!'" [It should be noted that Kane said that last part in a perfect Tony the Tiger voice.]

Young Tom soon discovered he could do almost any voice he heard—and he loved doing it. By the time he was 15, he was confident enough to start cold-calling local advertisers, offering his services as an announcer.

"The local commercials were horrendously bad," he recalls, "and I just thought it would be fun to hear myself on TV. It didn't occur to me that anybody got paid for it. Most turned me away, but I got a call back from the American Cancer Society's ad agency. I had called, basically saying, 'Your Public Service Announcement sounds like you put the microphone in front of the receptionist.' I was a teenager and had no tact, but it turns out that's exactly what had happened. They called me up and said, 'We understand you're willing to donate your time.'

"I was 15 years old, but I sounded like an adult on the phone," he continues. "I had to have my dad drive me to the studio, and of course, they walked up to him. He said, "No," and pointed at this pimply-faced teenager. The poor producer had to explain to his boss that this 15-year-old kid was the one he hired!"

The producers were even more skeptical when the "pimply teen" offered to read the script, "like the old man from the Pepperidge Farms commercials," he said, but their attitudes changed when the young upstart delivered a perfect, Wilford Brimley-esque performance in one take. "I wasn't trying to show off," he confesses. "I just thought it would be fun." Three days later, the same ad agency hired him to voice a cowboy in five more TV ads.

"By the time I went to college, I'd done probably a hundred commercials," Kane said, "and by the time I got out of college, I'd done several hundred. But I always wanted to do cartoons, and there's only one place those exist, and that's Los Angeles. So we made our way out there around 1985, and I was tremendously successful in every other aspect of voice-over work very quickly. But I couldn't get arrested when it came to cartoons. I auditioned and auditioned, and I think I was there for six years before I started landing anything. I'd really almost given up."

A LIFE CHANGING MOVIE!
It turned out that Kane's break came out of another passion from his formative years in Kansas—his love of Star Wars. "It was the last day of school in the ninth grade when Star Wars came out in 1977," he recalls, "and the world changed for me that day. Within 10 seconds, when that Star Destroyer came overhead, I just sat there with my mouth hanging open, going, 'Whoa!' I think I saw the movie 12 times. I took my mom, and then I

> **"I took my grandmother to see _Star Wars_. She said, 'Oh honey, I don't watch those types of movies,' and I said, 'Grandma, you will love this!'"**

FROM ACKBAR TO YULAREN
TOM KANE'S 11 GREATEST _STAR WARS_ VOICES

Admiral Ackbar
(_Star Wars_: Battlefront)

Bib Fortuna
(_Star Wars_: Demolition)

Boba Fett
(_Star Wars_: Demolition, Galactic Battleground and Jedi Knight: Jedi Academy)

Leebo (Shadows of the Empire)

Lobot (_Star Wars_: Demolition)

General Madine
(Rogue Squadron series)

Narrator
(_Star Wars_: The Clone Wars)

Nien Nunb
(_Star Wars_: X-Wing Alliance)

Vandar Tokare
(Knights of the Old Republic)

Yoda
(_Star Wars_: The Clone Wars, the movie and animated series; _Star Wars_: Clone Wars, the micro-series; and various games and toys)

Wullf Yularen
(_Star Wars_: The Clone Wars)

took my grandmother. She said, 'Oh honey, I don't watch those types of movies,' and I said, 'Grandma, you will love this,' and she did. When the other movies came out over the next several years, she went and saw them."

So Kane was thrilled when he finally got a job doing character voices for LucasArts. "Then the first time they hired me to do something for *Star Wars*," he said, "I sat there sort of just shaking my head, because to be a fan and find myself sitting in front of a script with the words *Star Wars* on it, and characters that I knew and loved, and here I am working for a guy that had an office up at Lucasfilm . . . I'm sitting there thinking, 'How did this happen?'"

It happened because Kane could seemingly do any voice in the *Star Wars* universe, as he proved over the course of the last dozen years doing voices for videogames, from classic voices heard in the *Star Wars* movies to brand new characters. Some of those new characters were still familiar, posing an even greater challenge. Kane had to come up with

BEYOND
STAR WARS

TOM KANE'S ANIMATION AND VOICE-OVER LEGACY

These are just a few selected characters from Tom Kane's extensive voice-ography:

H.O.M.E.R., *Iron Man* (1995-96)

Dr. Doom, *Spider-Man* (1997)

Dante, *Team Knight Rider* (1997-98)

Berry, *Johnny Bravo* (1997-2000)

Professor Utonium/Him, *The Powerpuff Girls* (1998-2005)

Darwin, The Wild Thornberrys (1998-2002)

Greco, *Heavy Gear: The Animated Series* (2001)

Gandalf, *Lord of the Rings: The Fellowship of the Ring* (videogame) (2002)

Lord Monkey Fist, *Kim Possible* (2002-2007)

Various Characters, *Duck Dodgers* (2003-2005)

Dean Cain, *The Adventures of Jimmy Neutron, Boy Genius* (2005)

Ultimos, *Ben 10* (2006)

Guard, *Shrek The Third* (2007)

Mr. Herriman, *Foster's Home for Imaginary Friends* (2004-2008)

Magneto, *Wolverine and the X-Men* (2008-2009)

Commissioner Gordon, Batman: Arkham Asylum (videogame) (2009)

the first-ever voice for previously-silent Lando-sidekick Lobot, as well as the sound of Vandar Tokare, one of only two other known members of Yoda's species, who soon returns in a new multi-player online game, *Star Wars*: The Old Republic.

"We had to come up with a voice for him," Kane says. "So we ended up basically doing Yoda but then I changed it slightly, and the thing we did to make it completely different is that he doesn't speak in 'Yodese,' he doesn't flop his words.'"

As time went by, Kane became entrusted with more major roles, such as filling in for Anthony Daniels as C-3PO for some games. "It's his voice," Kane insists. "I'm just caretaking it occasionally when he doesn't want to do the job or isn't available."

In contrast, Kane has pretty much inherited Yoda from Frank Oz, who originated the part in the *Star Wars* feature films but hasn't performed it since Episode III. Those are not small shoes to fill. Oz, who began his career as a puppeteer with Jim Henson's Muppets, has created and performed the voices for some of the most treasured characters in

our culture, including *Sesame Street*'s Cookie Monster, Grover, and Bert, and *The Muppet Show*'s Miss Piggy, Fozzie Bear, and Animal, among many others. Oz's Yoda captured the world's imagination since his first appearance in *The Empire Strikes Back*; could any actor even come close to that standard?

YODA THE ICON!

Kane admits that even though he had George Lucas' full confidence, the magnitude of the character can be a little intimidating.

"I look at it not just as a cool gig, which it is," he said, "but it is such an honor to be entrusted with something that iconic, with a voice that's known to the world. James Arnold Taylor, who is [the voice of] Obi-Wan, is now Fred Flintstone, and something we talk about is how honored we are to be caretaking these characters and their voices. It's not something we created, so even though it may become ours, it's on loan. I may be Yoda for another couple years or another 20 years, it's up to George, but for as long as it lasts, I'm just trying to do it the

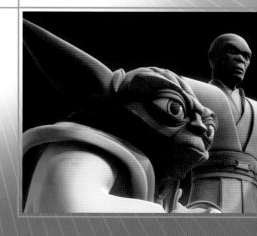

FROM LEFT TO RIGHT: Matt Lanter, Catherine Taber, James Arnold Taylor, Grey DeLisle, Tom Kane, George Lucas, Kevin Kiner, Ashley Eckstein, David Accord, Ian Abercrombie, Matthew Wood, Dee Bradley Baker

"I would love to do Darth Vader, but he's so hard to do!"

justice that it warrants and hope everyone's happy with it."

So far, so good. Kane not only continues to play Yoda, but is expanding his *Star Wars* repertoire with still more characters. In *Star Wars: The Clone Wars*, Kane also voices Admiral Wullf Yularen and provides the opening narration at the start of each episode.

Still, there is one *Star Wars* character Kane has said he could never play.

"I would love to do Darth Vader, but he's so hard to do," the actor admits. "There is a quality to James Earl Jones' voice that is just impossible to duplicate. My Vader is OK for a line or two, but it's not going to fly for any length of time."

YODA IS NUMBER ONE!

No worries, since there's no shortage of work for Tom Kane, both inside and out of the *Star Wars* universe. "I like Professor Utonium," he says of his *Powerpuff Girls* alter ego. "He's one of the favorite characters that I've done because he's a dad and I'm a dad, so I got to put a bit of myself into that role. I think cartoons are always going to be nearest and dearest to my heart, because they're fun to do, and they mean something to my kids."

Still, Kane makes it clear that, "Yoda has to be number one. Anytime it's a character who was important in the films, that would just add a little extra weight to me emotionally, because as soon as I hear the words and hear the voice—even if it's me doing it—it brings back the joy at seeing the movies."

Perhaps one day, some voice-over actor of the future will be taking over the role of Professor Utonium, or Darwin, or even Yoda—and when that day comes, we will all be wondering and hoping: Can this guy really do justice to the voice mastery of the one and only Tom Kane? ☮

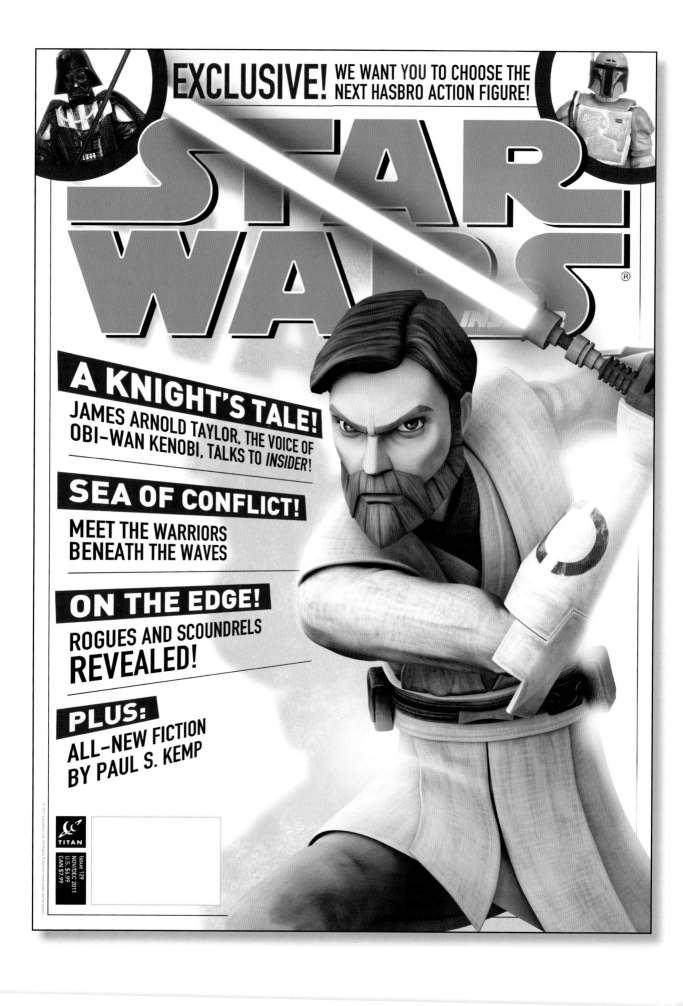

EXCLUSIVE! WE WANT YOU TO CHOOSE THE NEXT HASBRO ACTION FIGURE!

STAR WARS ®

A KNIGHT'S TALE!
JAMES ARNOLD TAYLOR, THE VOICE OF OBI-WAN KENOBI, TALKS TO *INSIDER*!

SEA OF CONFLICT!
MEET THE WARRIORS BENEATH THE WAVES

ON THE EDGE!
ROGUES AND SCOUNDRELS REVEALED!

PLUS:
ALL-NEW FICTION BY PAUL S. KEMP

TITAN

Issue 129
NOV/DEC 2011
U.S. $6.99
CAN $7.99

JAMES ARNOLD TAYLOR
OBI-WAN KENOBI

ISSUE 129
NOV/DEC 2011

The Millennium Falcon Owner's Workshop Manual, written by Ryder Windham and illustrated by Chris Trevas and Chris Reiff, published by Del Rey and Haynes in the U.K. (November)

Star Wars: The Old Republic MMORPG (massively multiplayer online role-playing game) released by Lucasarts and Electronic Arts (December)

Wildly cheerful and out going, James Arnold Taylor never fails to pop over to the *Star Wars Insider* booth at Celebration to say hi. His infectious personality, and positive outlook is genuinely inspiring, so he is the perfect choice to play the younger, perhaps slightly more playful Obi-Wan Kenobi. In fact, during the clone wars, Obi-Wan seems a lot more swashbuckling. However, when this interview was conducted, there was a real sense of Obi-Wan and the Jedi heading down a very dark path. That's what was so unique about *Star Wars: The Clone Wars*. No other franchise has used an animated series to expand on its mythology and with such impressive results, and Taylor was a major part of that.—**Jonathan Wilkins**

James Arnold Taylor (born July 22, 1969) is an American voice actor and author. He is best known for portraying Obi-Wan Kenobi in several Star Wars *projects; most significantly the* Clone Wars *micro-series and the* Star Wars: The Clone Wars *film and TV series.*

TAYLOR MADE

JAMES ARNOLD TAYLOR CAN MAKE THE PRESTIGIOUS CLAIM OF HAVING PLAYED OBI–WAN KENOBI LONGER THAN ANY OTHER ACTOR. WITH SEASON FOUR OF *STAR WARS: THE CLONE WARS* TAKING THE SHOW IN EXCITING NEW DIRECTIONS, HE TELLS US WHY THE CHARACTER IS THE ROCK AT THE CENTER OF THE DRAMA. INTERVIEW: JONATHAN WILKINS

Why do you think Obi-Wan is so popular?
His accent! And his charm! Actually, I think that the biggest reason is the prequels. The prequels kind of turned Obi-Wan into a leading man, even though the story is about Anakin and Darth Vader and the Skywalkers. I think that he had a new grace with Ewan McGregor, and now *The Clone Wars* has taken the character even further.

Obi-Wan constantly attempts to keep everybody on track, but he also tries to be realistic. You saw that in "The Citadel" episode in Season Three where they're losing clones left, right, and center. I remember when we were in the studio voicing that stuff, Dave [Filoni] kept telling me that Obi-Wan is the one who says we must move forward and we have to keep going. I had to strike a balance when recording those lines to show he has sympathy and heart for the clones, but at the same time he knows the mission. I think that sort of sums up the character.

He's strong when other characters don't necessarily know what to do, and he's a voice of reason.

What can we expect from Obi-Wan in Season Four?
There are some things in this season that took me by complete surprise. It's going to be an awesome season for Obi-Wan and the fans who follow him. The fans on Twitter and Facebook always say, "More Obi-Wan! More Obi-Wan!" Well, I think they'll definitely get a lot more Obi-Wan this season. Oh, there are a lot of things I want to tell you, but I just can't!

The drama got pretty intense last season. Is that something you anticipated when you signed up to do the show?
You know, I think it's something I hoped for.

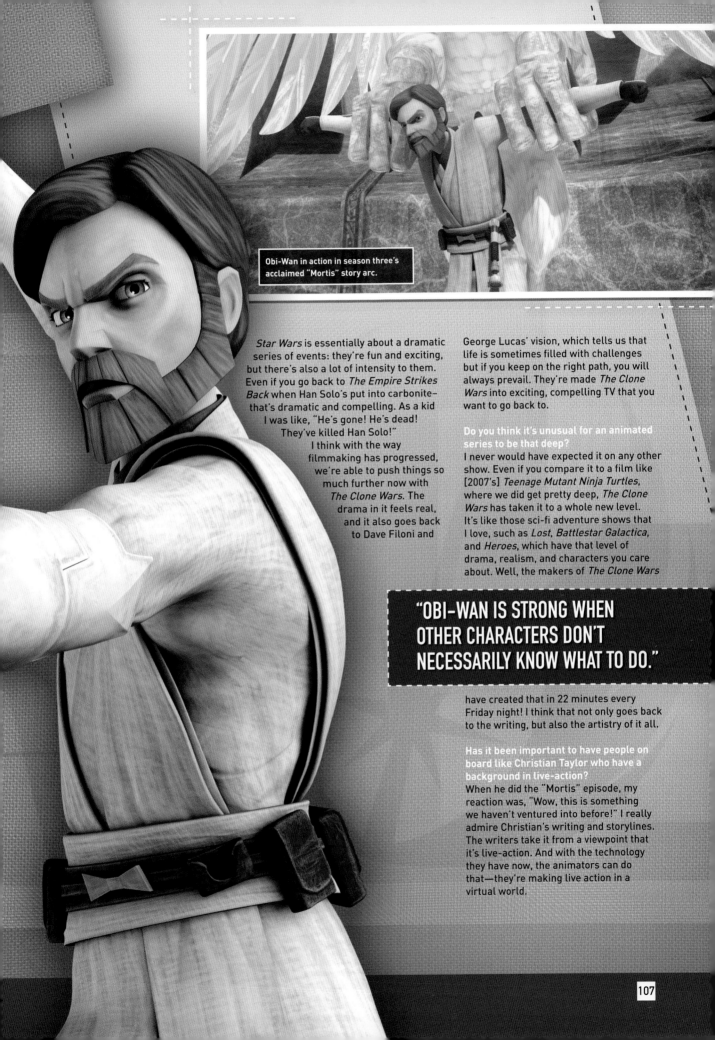

Obi-Wan in action in season three's acclaimed "Mortis" story arc.

Star Wars is essentially about a dramatic series of events: they're fun and exciting, but there's also a lot of intensity to them. Even if you go back to *The Empire Strikes Back* when Han Solo's put into carbonite– that's dramatic and compelling. As a kid I was like, "He's gone! He's dead! They've killed Han Solo!" I think with the way filmmaking has progressed, we're able to push things so much further now with *The Clone Wars*. The drama in it feels real, and it also goes back to Dave Filoni and George Lucas' vision, which tells us that life is sometimes filled with challenges but if you keep on the right path, you will always prevail. They're made *The Clone Wars* into exciting, compelling TV that you want to go back to.

Do you think it's unusual for an animated series to be that deep?
I never would have expected it on any other show. Even if you compare it to a film like [2007's] *Teenage Mutant Ninja Turtles*, where we did get pretty deep, *The Clone Wars* has taken it to a whole new level. It's like those sci-fi adventure shows that I love, such as *Lost*, *Battlestar Galactica*, and *Heroes*, which have that level of drama, realism, and characters you care about. Well, the makers of *The Clone Wars*

> ## "OBI-WAN IS STRONG WHEN OTHER CHARACTERS DON'T NECESSARILY KNOW WHAT TO DO."

have created that in 22 minutes every Friday night! I think that not only goes back to the writing, but also the artistry of it all.

Has it been important to have people on board like Christian Taylor who have a background in live-action?
When he did the "Mortis" episode, my reaction was, "Wow, this is something we haven't ventured into before!" I really admire Christian's writing and storylines. The writers take it from a viewpoint that it's live-action. And with the technology they have now, the animators can do that—they're making live action in a virtual world.

Obi-Wan: Wise and always primed for action, even against a surprise opponent!

Obi-Wan and Asajj Ventress's epic confrontations are one of many highlights of the show.

When do you get the script during the recording process, and what kind of work do you do before you even start recording?
It's changed a bit over the last season. Some of that comes from working on such a tight schedule, but it's also due to the top secret nature of it. Generally speaking, you'd get scripts 24 hours in advance, but now we get them when we go to the session.

But we do get a chance to go through everything before the session starts. Dave sits down with us all as a cast and goes through the story, and then talks to every person there, whether it's a guest star or whether it's Matt [Lanter], Ashley [Eckstein] or myself, who are there every week. He takes his time with each person and gives us pictures or descriptions of what's happening, and provides background on the episodes either side of the one we're recording. It really helps.

That approach also adds to our ability to change things. Dave might go, "Oh that doesn't really feel like Obi-Wan. What if he said this instead?" Or I might say, "This is a great line as it's written but when I say it, it doesn't come out right." There's a freedom for us all to act as we might on camera.

The process of recording is intense, though. As voice actors, we really have to think on our toes. We run through a scene three to eight times on average, and try to make it different each time.

Prequel producer Rick McCallum says that a hint of romance between Padmé and Obi-Wan was cut from *Revenge of the Sith*. Is that something you'd like to see in *The Clone Wars*?
(Laughs) Cat [Taber, who plays Padmé] and

THE CHANGING FACE OF OBI-WAN KENOBI

SIR ALEC GUINNESS
Appeared in: *Star Wars* (1977); *The Empire Strikes Back* (1980); *Return of the Jedi* (1983).

EWAN MCGREGOR
Appeared in: *The Phantom Menace* (1999); *Attack of the Clones* (2002); *Revenge of the Sith* (2005).

JAMES ARNOLD TAYLOR
Appeared in: *Clone Wars* micro-series (2003); *The Clone Wars* (2008—present); Battlefront II videogame (2005); Revenge of the Sith videogame (2005).

DAVID DAVIES
Appeared: *Star Wars*: Galactic Battlegrounds (2001) and *Star Wars*: Rogue Squadron II: Rogue Leader (2001).

TIM OMUNDSON
Appeared: *Star Wars*: Rogue Squadron III: Rebel Strike (2003).

BERNARD "BUNNY" BEHRENS
Appeared: Radio dramatizations of *Star Wars* (1981); *The Empire Strikes Back* (1983); *Return of the Jedi* (1996).

Ewan MacGregor

Sir Alec Guinness

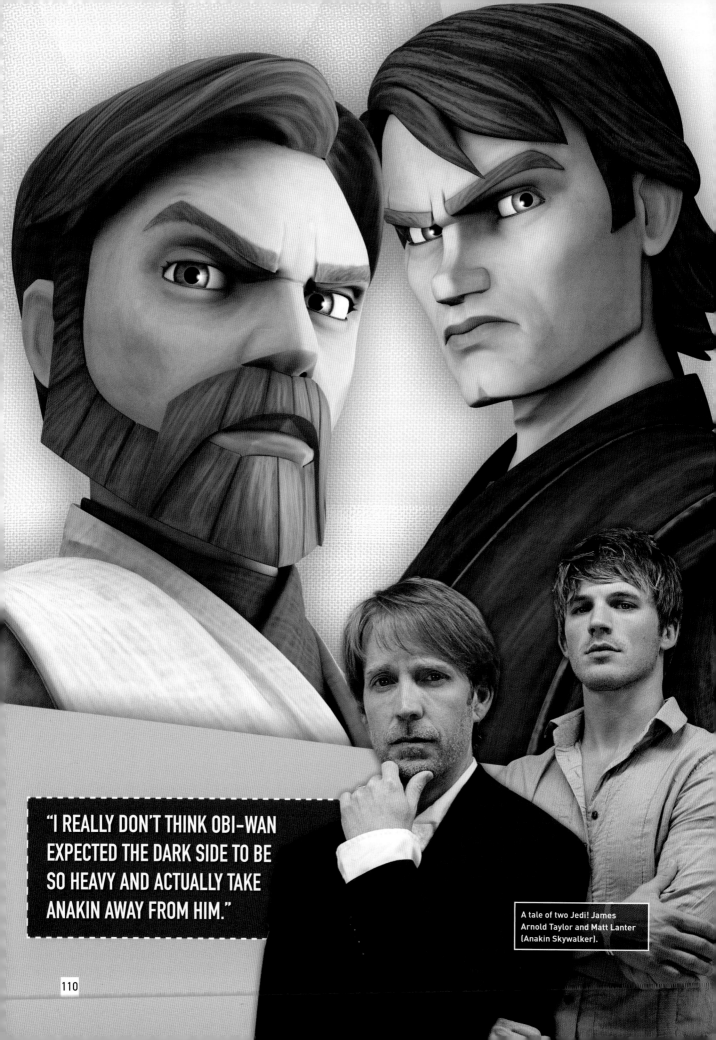

"I REALLY DON'T THINK OBI-WAN EXPECTED THE DARK SIDE TO BE SO HEAVY AND ACTUALLY TAKE ANAKIN AWAY FROM HIM."

A tale of two Jedi! James Arnold Taylor and Matt Lanter (Anakin Skywalker).

I are such good friends and we always joke around with Dave and say, "Come on, man, we've got to see a [romantic] episode like that!" In Episodes I and II, Obi-Wan thinks she's a politician like Palpatine, and doesn't buy what she says. But then somewhere down the line there's a connection and a bond that's made between them. In the show, we do get a chance to explore what happened and why they're closer by Episode III.

Obi-Wan is quite straight-laced. Do you ever wish you could play more comedy with him?
Ewan [McGregor] did have some great moments, especially in the elevator scene in Episode III; Obi-Wan was having fun! You could see that playful nature in his relationship with Anakin—you could see they're like brothers, not father and son. We do get some of those moments in *The Clone Wars* now and again, too. Several times each season, Obi-Wan has a quip that just cuts through and you're like, "Oh behave, Obi-Wan!" So it's definitely there, but it would be fun to see a bit more.

I play Plo Koon as well as Obi-Wan, and they're very serious parts. I'm so honored to play these two Jedi because they hold such weight in the storyline, but it would

be fun to have a character who could go a bit more crazy every once in a while, as well!

He has an intriguing relationship with Asajj Ventress.
Oh yes, there's a lot of playfulness between those characters. I mean, they really get to flirt! Fans often ask me: "So what's the deal between Obi-Wan and Ventress?" (Adopts Obi-Wan voice) "Well, I can't possibly say...."

Also, Nika Futterman [who plays Ventress] is such a fantastic actress. In fact, the very first scene we recorded was the one you see in *The Clone Wars* film, where she and I are having our battle. She brings me up to a different level as an actor.

You also had some great banter with the Duchess Satine in the "Duchess of Mandalore." Was that as much fun to play as it was to watch?
It was. Anna Graves, who plays the Duchess, is such a talented actress. She and I have done promo work in the past, and for us to have a good old battle of words is great!

I love the comedy in their relationship. Like that bit in the second part of the story, when Obi-Wan is hanging upside down and about to be crushed, and he says: "I'm a little tired up here!" But there's also a love between those characters, too. I think that's the main thing—we joke with the ones that we love. Obi-Wan has a heart for all of the characters, and I try to keep that in mind when I'm doing it, so it doesn't come across as too mean or snarky.

How do you think Obi-Wan's relationship with Anakin is progressing? Do you think he's at all aware of Anakin's dark side slowly coming to the front?
I try to keep that in mind, especially in the last season when Mortis appeared. It's one of those parts where you're like, "How do I play this?" Because right now we're in between Episodes II and III; I know what happens in III, but I can't let that affect how I play him here. I think that he feels—and this is the way I play

it—that [the attraction to the dark side] is always going to be a part of Anakin and any other Jedi. But Obi-Wan knows the strength of Anakin and thinks he'll overcome it.

I don't think Obi-Wan expected anything that happened in Episodes III to V. I think he was so trusting in Anakin and the Force; he had hope and faith. I really don't think he expected the dark side to be so heavy and actually take Anakin away from him. And of course that's a pain that we see in Episode III.

And it also reflects his trust in Qui-Gon.
That's a good point. I always think about that. I mean, we always think of Yoda as his teacher and instructor, but really the father to him was Qui-Gon. When we had the surprise of Qui-Gon appearing in the "Mortis" trilogy, I was like, "Oh this is so awesome!" And what a great honor to have a scene with Liam Neeson!

When we did that scene, I actually, very subtly, youthed my voice up a little. I went back to *The Phantom Menace*, watched that a lot, and gave the voice a slightly lighter and softer tone. Because Obi-Wan reverts back to when he was younger. I thought he would be very off-guard and revert back to when he was with his master.

Did you get to meet Liam Neeson?
I didn't. He was in New York when we did it, and he recorded his part there. It's funny; that is such a heavy part of voice-acting. I've been able to work with just about everybody in showbiz today, but usually the scenes are recorded completely separately so I never get to meet them. Take Patrick Stewart and Samuel L. Jackson—I've been in five or six projects with each of them, and yet we've never met. Even though most of our scenes feature the two of us having conversations! One of these days it would be fun to meet them, but alas, that's the work of a voice actor!

If you could play a character from the movies who we haven't seen yet, who would it be?
I'd love to see a young Han Solo, but I know that's not possible! It would be interesting doing Uncle Owen—we haven't seen him [in *The Clone Wars*], but we know he's kicking around right now. That's a voice that would be fun to explore. I've always felt that the character goes deeper than we ever got to see. I'd love to learn more about exactly what he knows. That would be fun! ☻

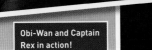

Obi-Wan and Captain Rex in action!

ASAJJ VENTRESS IN AN ALL-NEW TALE, INSIDE!

STAR WARS
INSIDER

MYSTERIES OF THE FORCE!
How the *Star Wars* prequels enhanced the mythos!

WIN A
STAR WARS
THE FORCE AWAKENS
STORMTROOPER
HOT WHEELS CAR!

JEDI REBEL

Actress Ashley Eckstein on the return of Ahsoka Tano in *Star Wars Rebels*!

ISSUE #159
UK £3.99
AUG/SEPT 2015

TITAN

ASHLEY ECKSTEIN
AHSOKA TANO

ISSUE 159
AUG/SEP 2015

Ashley Eckstein and her character Ahsoka Tano are a bona fide *Star Wars* success story, but when *Star Wars: The Clone Wars* reached its conclusion it seemed that her journey was at an untimely end. I remember speaking with her at Celebration Europe in Germany and she seemed resigned to the fact that Ahsoka's journey was over.

But, of course, there was more to come, and as the first season of *Star Wars Rebels* reached its conclusion, Ahsoka was revealed to be alive and well. It's true to say that in *Star Wars* nobody truly stays dead! From Obi-Wan's surprise return to encourage Luke, to Darth Maul's miraculous resurrection, the *Star Wars* saga has always retained the ability to surprise. Even now, with Ahsoka seemingly lost to us once again, I wouldn't be surprised if she returns someday, somehow.—**Jonathan Wilkins**

Maria Ashley Eckstein (born September 22, 1981) came to prominence as Muffy on the Disney Channel sitcom That's So Raven, *before winning film roles in* Sydney White *(2007) and* Alice Upside Down *(2007). In 2010, Eckstein set up the company Her Universe to provide sci-fi and cult apparel to a female audience.*

ASHLEY ECKSTEIN, THE VOICE OF AHSOKA TANO, ON THE RETURN OF THE CHARACTER TO *STAR WARS REBELS*, CELEBRATION ANAHEIM, AND PROVIDING FASHION INSPIRATION FOR KATHLEEN KENNEDY. INTERVIEW BY AMY RATCLIFFE

Star Wars Insider: *Star Wars* Celebration Anaheim opened with *The Force Awakens* panel, and Kathleen Kennedy walked onto the stage wearing Her Universe's lightsaber T-shirt. Did you know that was happening?

Ashley Eckstein: No, I had no idea that Kathleen Kennedy was going to wear our T-shirt [laughs]. It was such an exciting surprise. I did know that she bought it, but I thought that she was wearing it to dinner the night before. So I thought that she had already worn it and the last thing I expected was for her to walk out on stage in our tee. It's like when Kate Middleton wears something and then everyone goes crazy for it. I'm so grateful, and I now call it the Kathleen Kennedy shirt! I feel like she is an icon. Not only is she a fangirl icon, but I feel like she's just an icon for all fans. And if you see Kathleen Kennedy wearing something, naturally in your head you think, *I now have to own a white blazer to pair with that T-shirt because she looks so fantastic.*

Her Universe offered several new items and styles at Celebration. How did the new pin-up dresses go over?
It was great. The fans were incredibly supportive and luckily we had a dressing room at the show. We had long lines, but everyone was patient. This was our first foray into a lot more fashion-forward designs, so we learned a lot and definitely got everyone's feedback—good and bad—and we're going to be improving on that. It was a really exciting con; the lightsaber skirt and cardigans were the most popular items.

AHSOKA TANO

From left to right: Ashley Eckstein; Ahsoka emerges from her Master's shadow; the beginning: Ahsoka's debut appearance in the *Star Wars: The Clone Wars* movie (2008)

> "I SAW THE *REBELS* PREMIERE EPISODE FOR THE FIRST TIME IN A ROOM WITH A COUPLE OF THOUSAND PEOPLE!"

What are some of the top highlights of the rest of your Celebration experience? The *Star Wars Rebels* panel with everyone—especially the surprise appearance of Dee [Bradley Baker] and I on stage and everyone finding out that Captain Rex was coming back. Dee and I were standing backstage when Rex appeared on the trailer and just hearing the crowd roar at that moment was so exciting. It was so electric, and then to walk out on stage together with him was incredible.

And then there was the *Rebels* premiere. That was the first time I'd seen the episode and to watch it with a couple thousand people in the room for the first time was really just surreal.

The third highlight was the Ahsoka Lives Day. It was so special to see how the fans still love Ahsoka and support her, and to see fans dressed as Ahsoka just melted my heart. Honestly, I got goose bumps at the turnout.

How hard was it for you to keep the return of Ahsoka under your hat?
It was a hard secret to keep. I've known the secret for about a year now, and it's just been so tough because I haven't lied to the fans, but I can't tell the truth so what do you really say? When friends would ask me over and over again, "Is Ahsoka going to be in *Rebels*? Are we going to see Ahsoka again?" I would just have to say, "Well, you know, she's still alive. It's kind of too soon to tell. You know, they're still writing *Rebels*. Who knows? Maybe we'll see her one day."

But once Fulcrum came into the storyline, it was harder to be vague. The fans— who are so fantastic— pitched up Fulcrum's voice and said, "Okay, that sounds like Ashley and the way that she speaks!" I pretty much went into hiding after that because I didn't know what to say. I kind of avoided interviews, all podcasts, really all social media about the subject, until after the finale aired because I didn't know what to say about it, and I didn't want to lie about it.

She's not the only character from *Clone Wars* jumping to *Rebels*. The season two trailer that premiered at Celebration showed Captain Rex and Hondo Ohnaka. What does it mean to you to see these characters continue to live in *Rebels*?
I'm also a huge fan of these characters in *Star Wars* and so, as a fan, I became so invested in them. We spent six seasons on *The Clone Wars* getting to know these characters so deeply—we really did. They're animated characters, but we became emotionally attached to them. I can't say enough about Captain Rex and what he means, but also Hondo is a personal favorite of mine. So for

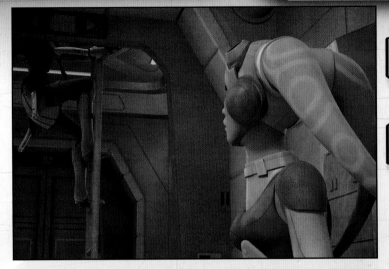

The Clone Wars to end like it did, kind of on a cliffhanger and not knowing where these characters ended up, it means so much for them to come back in *Rebels* because we need more. We need more of their storylines, we need to know where they went and what they've been doing, what happened to them.

Rex and Ahsoka have quite a history. What kind of relationship do they have now?
They have a bond like family. They really spent so much time side-by-side fighting in *Clone Wars*. I think Ahsoka has such a special bond with Rex because he was kind of like a mentor in a way, along with Anakin—even though she said in the show, "So, if you are a captain and I'm a Jedi, then technically I outrank you, right?" Rex quickly put her in her place and said, "Well, experience outranks everything," and I think she respected him from day one for that and admired that she had to earn his respect. I think along with Anakin and the rest of the gang, it's like an older brother and a family member. So they have a really, really tight bond and we don't know what happened between them after she walked away from the Clone Wars, but we do know that they're both still alive, and hopefully we'll get to find out more about what they've been doing since.

Opposite page, from left: Ezra and Ahsoka make battle plans; the return of the (former) Jedi!

This page, left from the top: The iconic moment "Fulcrum's" identity was finally revealed to the *Ghost* crew!

Left: Ashley models a handy Wicket bag!

This page, right, from top: Hera and Ahsoka; Ashley models the T-shirt as worn by Kathleen Kennedy at Celebration Anaheim; Ahsoka in action on the bridge of the *Ghost*.

Opposite page, left to right: Ahsoka's experiences have made her a much tougher Togruta! Bonding with Chopper!

Both Rex and Ahsoka were close with Anakin Skywalker, and Darth Vader is in the picture on *Rebels* along with them. Is Ahsoka aware of Darth Vader as a presence in the galaxy?

Darth Vader is a newer presence to the rebels. And, what else can I say to that? [laughs] I can't say much about Ahsoka and Vader and what she knows and what she doesn't know. But I do know that once Dave Filoni told me that if Ahsoka and Darth Vader were to eventually confront each other, that it probably wouldn't be a good thing for Ahsoka. Dave said on the *Rebels* panel that, obviously, it's a natural progression for her story. *If* that does happen—and I can honestly answer you with *if* because I don't know that part of her story— I fear for her because of that looming advice Dave Filoni once gave me.

If Vader is aware of who Ahsoka is, he probably wouldn't like having such a strong reminder of the person he used to be around.

Absolutely. He is the *most* powerful, and as powerful as I think Ahsoka is—and of course I am biased—it's still Darth Vader [laughs]. I don't know how well she would fair. So we'll see.

We know Ahsoka is helping the rebels fight back against the Empire. Will we learn more about her specific role within the budding rebellion?

Ahsoka will continue to remain a mysterious character. She's a recurring character so she's not going to be a main character in every single episode. And Ahsoka has questions that she needs answered, so we'll see her, but then she's also going to be on her own journey getting her questions answered.

> "I THINK KANAN AND EZRA HAVE A BOND THAT IS LIKE AHSOKA AND ANAKIN'S, IN THAT IT IS UNBREAKABLE."

We saw Ahsoka walk away from the Jedi lifestyle, but she likely received more training than Kanan. Will we see Ezra wanting to learn from her?

I think Kanan and Ezra have a bond that is like Ahsoka and Anakin's in that it is unbreakable, and that can't be replaced by Ahsoka. I think how I would almost describe it is how Ahsoka was with Obi-Wan. Ahsoka and Anakin were really close, but Obi-Wan was this wise adviser that Ahsoka almost cowered to a little bit, because there was so much respect—like he was the master to the master, if that makes sense. There was like an extra level of respect there; she was always on her best behavior around Obi-Wan. She always watched her manners and Ps and Qs, and she wasn't too snippy with Obi-Wan. I almost think Ahsoka will be viewed by Ezra with a sense of reverence of, "She is this master to the master,"

"THERE ARE SO MANY
LESSONS I'VE LEARNED
FROM AHSOKA. I OFTEN
THINK, *WHAT WOULD
AHSOKA DO?*"

essentially. Ahsoka's not that, but I'm just
saying, Ezra has more of a friendly relationship
with Kanan with the banter and the wisecracks.

She is the mentor now, and, in some ways, so
are you with the *Rebels* cast. What has it been
like to be a veteran in both areas?
It's so funny because I just experienced that at
Celebration. This was the first Celebration for
the whole cast of *Rebels*. And so backstage
I was giving them advice like, "Okay, here's
what's going to happen, and here's what we are
going to do and here is what to expect!" They all
had several questions. Right before they walked
out on stage for the panel, they were like, "Oh my
gosh, we can't believe all the fans out there," and
they were nervous. It's definitely like life imitates
art. I felt like Ahsoka—I was able to provide
advice because this was my fourth Celebration.

Ahsoka has come such a long way from the character we first met in 2008. Have you learned any lessons from her?
There are so many lessons that I've learned from Ahsoka. Sometimes it feels silly to say that this animated character has taught us so much, but she really has. I look up to her. I often think, *What would Ahsoka do?* I feel like she has such a good heart and such a good moral compass that she'll always choose what's right, and I often keep that in mind. But I think with Ahsoka in *Rebels*— she's now back with a sense of confidence. It's almost like when we go to school for so many years and then when we graduate, we're out in the real world. It's like Ahsoka is now out in the real world, and we now see her in her job and she is very confident in it. I think that's what we can take from her right now in *Rebels*: Just be confident in what you're doing and go forward with the story. ☸

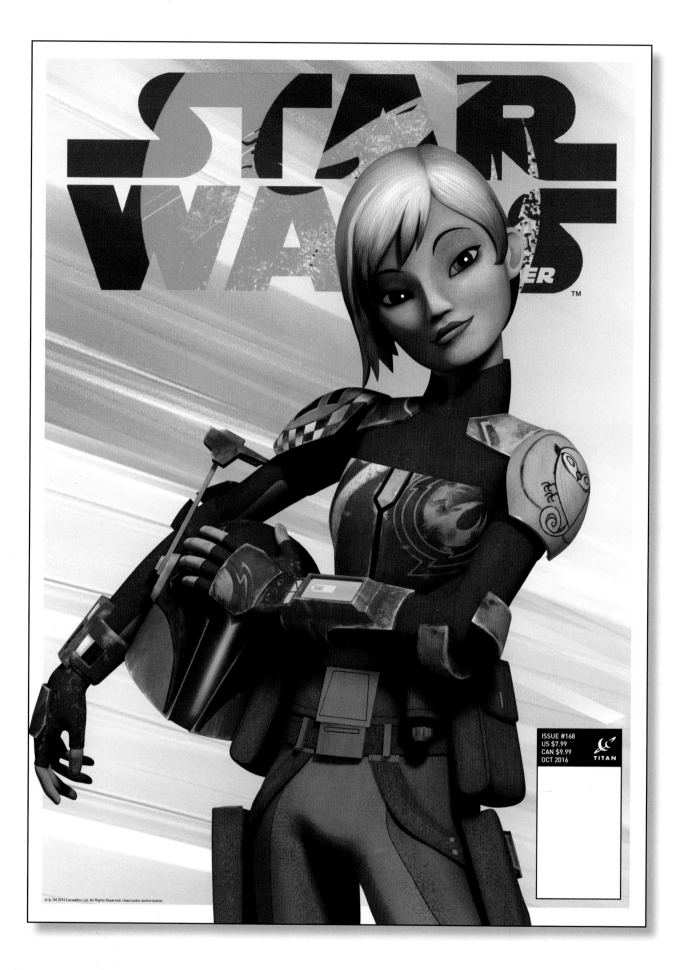

ISSUE #168
US $7.99
CAN $9.99
OCT 2016

TITAN

MAD MAGAZINE
USE THE FARCE

ISSUE 168
OCTOBER 2016

THIS MONTH, FAR, FAR AWAY....

Star Wars: Ahsoka young adult novel by E. K. Johnston, published by Disney Lucasfilm Press

Star Wars Propaganda: A History of Persuasive Art in the Galaxy written by Pablo Hidalgo, published by Becker and Mayer

The Amazing Book of Star Wars by David Fentiman, published by DK

MAD magazine has been poking fun at George Lucas' creation since day one, and all with the creator's blessing. We fans may take *Star Wars* very seriously, but it's always good to find the humor in the saga, too. George Lucas' fondness for *MAD* was obvious way back when he hired legendary *MAD* artist Mort Drucker to design the poster for *American Graffiti* in 1973. Later, Lucas even wrote the foreword for *MAD about Star Wars*, a collection of the best *Star Wars* send-ups from the magazine. It's a well-chosen title. To devote so much time and energy making fun of one subject, you really have to be crazy about it!—**Jonathan Wilkins**

USE THE FARCE

HOOHAH! *STAR WARS INSIDER* TAKES A LOOK AT THE LIGHTER SIDE OF *STAR WARS*, AS SEEN THROUGH THE EYES OF *MAD* MAGAZINE. WORDS: ARIE KAPLAN

MAD magazine might not be the first thing that springs to mind when it comes to *Star Wars*, but whenever a new *Star Wars* movie or TV show has debuted, *MAD* has always been there to parody it. That's been the case ever since the beloved humor publication spoofed *A New Hope* in *MAD* #196 (January 1978). In fact, by 2007 there were enough MAD *Star Wars* spoofs to fill a book—namely the Del Rey collection *MAD About Star Wars*, authored by former Lucasfilm employee (and then-*MAD* editor) Jonathan Bresman.

During the past 40 years, *MAD* has skewered the saga so frequently that—as of this writing—the last four issues of the magazine (up to and including *MAD* #540, August 2016) have all included at least one article or comic strip lampooning *The Force Awakens*. And, in its ongoing quest to make fun of all things *Star Wars*, *MAD* has used the galaxy far, far away to satirize everything from politics to commercialism. Just as the Jedi are encouraged to use the Force, the writers, cartoonists, and editors at *MAD* have consistently used the Farce.

As George Lucas mentions in his foreword to *MAD About Star Wars*: "I grew up in an agricultural town in the 1950s and 1960s, which was not exactly the place for questioning authority. But then *MAD* magazine came along." He goes on to say that, by satirizing everything in the adult world, the irreverent humor publication showed him, "more often than not, the emperor, as it were, had no clothes."

This revelation—that the way things really are and the way they're presented to the public can be two separate things —had a profound effect on Lucas. It made him realize that if he wanted to see the status quo change, he had to make that change himself. Indeed, he's spent the bulk of his filmmaking career making movies about characters who fight to change the status quo, such as Luke Skywalker and Indiana Jones. As a way of paying homage to his childhood influence, Lucas hired legendary *MAD* cartoonist Mort Drucker to draw the poster art for his 1973 film *American Graffiti*.

THE OFFICIAL
STORMTROOPER
RECRUITMENT PAMPHLET

JOIN THE FIRST ORDER!

SEE THE
GALAXY! SERVE YOUR
MASTER! ENJOY AMAZING
BENEFITS!

there was an audience for such knowing references. But *MAD* writers were (and still are) different. They, alongside *MAD*'s illustrators and editors, have always added extra layers and details that a reader might only catch after reading a particular piece for the third or fourth time. For *MAD*, it is all about the details.

THE EMPIRE STRIKES BLECCH

According to Bresman, this attention to detail is a key reason why *MAD*'s *Star Wars* parodies have always worked so well as both parody and satire. They were written and illustrated by people who understood and admired the *Star Wars* saga. "There was kind of an interesting dynamic going on," Bresman reveals. "Because George

COVER STARS

MAD MAGAZINE HAS LAMPOONED *STAR WARS* ON NUMEROUS OCCASIONS OVER THE YEARS. HERE ARE SOME OF THE FUNNIEST EDITIONS!

Alfred as Darth Vader, *MAD* #196, January 1978

The *MAD Star Wars* Musical, *MAD* #203, December 1978

Alfred as Yoda, *MAD* #220, January 1981

Mr. T as Darth Vader and Alfred as Wicket, *MAD* #242, October 1983

Alfred as Jabba the Hutt, *MAD* #354, February 1997

Star Wars Characters' Bodies Spelling Out "*Star Wars*" *MAD Star Wars* Spectacular, summer 1999

Collector's Covers Parodying the Episode I Poster, *MAD* #383, July 1999

Alfred as Darth Maul, *MAD* #368 September 1999

Collector's Covers Parodying *Attack of the Clones*, *MAD* #419, July 2002

Alfred as Emperor Palpatine, *MAD* #454, June 2005

Alfred as a First Order stormtrooper, *MAD* #532 April 2015

Over the years, Lucas has enjoyed *MAD*'s constant skewering of the *Star Wars* universe. To Jonathan Bresman, this makes perfect sense. After all, the first issue of *MAD* was published in 1952, when Lucas was in elementary school. "George is of the *MAD* generation," Bresman explains. "*MAD* was on the same wavelength as ILM and George were."

Bresman points out the article "The *Star Wars* Log" (MAD #230, April 1982) as evidence of this harmony. Written by longtime *MAD* scribe Frank Jacobs and illustrated by Harry North, the feature is a fictional "top secret" file, ostensibly from the desk of George Lucas himself, detailing what the remaining films in the *Star Wars* saga are going to be about (it was published after *Empire*, but before *Return of the Jedi*). It includes the following passage: "Both Boba Fett and Jabba the Hut [sic] were once comrades of Darth Vader, and this is brought out in our ninth film, "Yessir, That's My Boba" (No. 4 in the series). We find out that Luke Skywalker's lightsaber was once recharged by Boba Fett's father, who we

suspect might be Chewbacca." As you can see, Jacobs accidentally predicted the eventual appearance of Boba Fett's father!

Jacobs' unintentional prescience isn't lost on Bresman. "Even though Jacobs is joking, he anticipated a lot of the prequels. He has stuff in the article about the Force being Luke's father, which kind of pre-dates the virgin birth of Anakin. And Jacobs has all this stuff about clones." Oddly enough, when "The *Star Wars* Log" brings up the subject of clones, Jacobs even writes that they will appear in "No. 2 in the series," which will be titled "Send in the Clones!"

In retrospect, it's amazing how much research Frank Jacobs did while writing "The *Star Wars* Log." He took the time to correctly name-check planets such as Alderaan, and though he misspells Chewbacca's homeworld as "Kazhyyyk," he must be given credit for even including a reference to Kashyyyk in the first place. Most comedy writers in the 1980s would not have attempted that level of accuracy when writing a "mere spoof," especially since—in that pre-internet era—they didn't know that

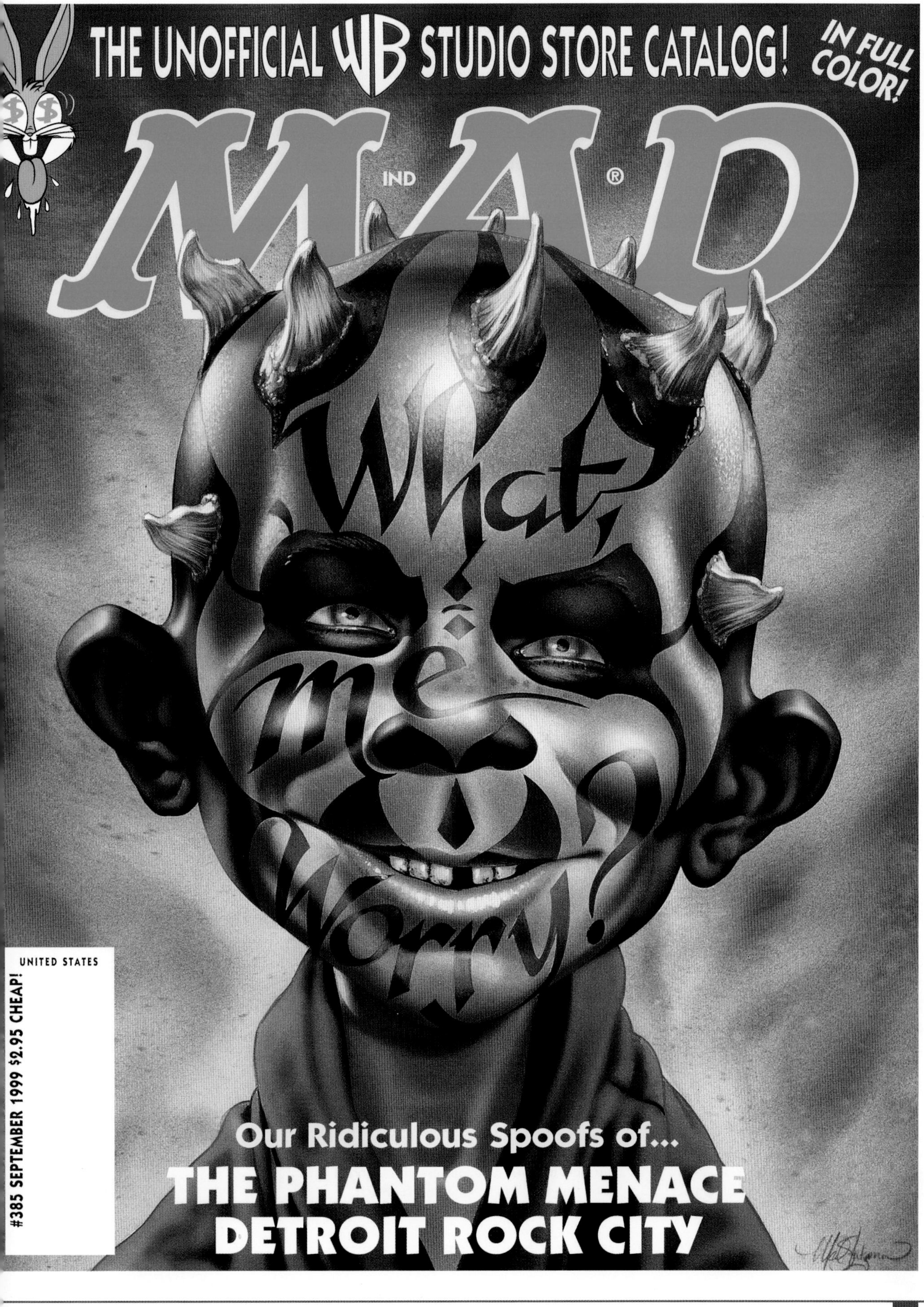

THE UNOFFICIAL WB STUDIO STORE CATALOG! IN FULL COLOR!

MAD
IND ®

What, me worry!

UNITED STATES

#385 SEPTEMBER 1999 $2.95 CHEAP!

Our Ridiculous Spoofs of...
THE PHANTOM MENACE
DETROIT ROCK CITY

and all his Industrial Light and Magic (ILM) colleagues sort of imbibed the *MAD* sensibility (while growing up); and MAD, in turn, is parodying something created by people who imbibed that sensibility. So they've got this great feedback loop going."

Bresman sees this "feedback loop" flowing through many of the *MAD Star Wars* parodies that have been published during the past four decades. The parody of *Return of the Jedi*, "Star Bores: Rehash of the Jeti," (*MAD* #242, October 1983), is a prime example. Written by Dick DeBartolo and illustrated by Mort Drucker, the piece opens with a group shot of the *Star Wars* cast of characters, in which Lando Calrissian is surrounded by Ewoks, as well as the dwarves from Disney's *Snow White and the Seven Dwarves*, and much-loved Muppets Kermit the Frog and Fozzie Bear.

The drawings of the Muppets in general, and Fozzie in particular, were a reference to Yoda being played by Frank Oz, who also played Fozzie Bear. "*MAD* draws in all the aspects of pop culture that are floating around out there when creating the parodies," Bresman explains, "which is kind of what George was doing when constructing the *Star Wars* movies. He was drawing on *Flash Gordon*, he was drawing on Frank Oz and the Muppets, and he was drawing on the fairytale tradition. So [*MAD* and George Lucas] were sort of eating the *Lady and the Tramp* spaghetti from opposite ends, and coming closer together in this great pop-cultural kiss."

Part of that "great pop-cultural kiss" is the fact that, beginning with that January 1978 parody of *A New Hope* ("Star Roars," written by Larry Siegel and Dick DeBartolo, and illustrated by Harry North), *MAD* artists started putting some very specific details into the asteroid fields they were depicting. They had no way of knowing it, but the ILM artists were putting similar details into the special effects sequences of the actual *Star Wars* films.

"If you look at Mort Drucker's asteroid fields [in his parodies of *The Empire Strikes Back* and *Return of the Jedi*], you'll find shoes and belt-buckles and baseballs and stuff like that," says Bresman. "Drucker didn't realize it, but if you look at the DVD commentary on all those movies, ILM was doing the same stuff. They have potatoes and shoes and all kinds of random debris in there."

Bresman attributes this to *Star Wars* and *MAD* being similarly layered with details.

MAD's first editor, Harvey Kurtzman, was known for drawing detailed thumbnail sketches for all of the *MAD* stories he wrote or edited, often going so far as drawing tissue paper overlays for his artists to follow. The artists he worked with, such as Will Elder, sometimes compared Kurtzman to a film director in that he would fully pre-visualize and "direct" every panel and every scene of the stories he was writing and editing.

Kurtzman left *MAD* in 1955, when the magazine was three years old, and the acerbic humor publication has changed and evolved quite a bit since then. However, one thing that has remained constant is its use of tiny background details and its obsession with accuracy. A *MAD* parody must resemble

the original work it is parodying in every possible way. So it is not surprising that Bresman sees parallels between George Lucas and Harvey Kurtzman. "Lucasfilm has this very hand-crafted ethic to it, in the same way that *MAD* does," Bresman states. "George would hire these world-class draftspeople and these world-class designers, and he'd pre-visualize every scene. It's kind of like the film version of the way Kurtzman worked with Elder and the others." It's fitting that one of Kurtzman's best-known *MAD* stories was a parody of the newspaper strip *Flash Gordon* ("Flesh Garden," written by Kurtzman and illustrated by Wally Wood, from *MAD* #11, May 1954]. *Flash Gordon* was, of course, one of Lucas' biggest inspirations when creating *Star Wars*.

THE FURSHLUGINNER AWAKENS

But George Lucas isn't the only *Star Wars* filmmaker who's a *MAD* fan. J.J. Abrams is a devotee of the magazine as well. In fact, Abrams has visited the *MAD* offices in New York City, and he wrote the foreword to the 2007 book *Spy Vs. Spy 2: The Joke and Dagger Files*, by David Shayne (a collection of *MAD*'s "Spy Vs. Spy" comic strips, which chronicle the pantomimed, slapstick escapades of two secret agents). Since Abrams created the secret agent-themed television series *Alias*, he was a natural choice to pen the foreword to the book.

Speaking of Abrams, *MAD*'s parody of *The Force Awakens*, entitled "Star Bores: The Snores Awaken," appeared in *MAD* #539 (June 2016). Written by David Richards and illustrated by Tom Richmond, it begins with J.J. Abrams and frequent collaborator Greg Grunberg (Snap Wexley in *The Force Awakens*) discussing some critics' complaints about the film. After numerous well-placed satirical swipes, it ends with Rey encountering a mysterious, hooded man in Jedi robes, who removes his hood to reveal... George Lucas! It's a nice twist ending that comments on the *Star Wars* franchise itself, which was initially created by the "Jedi Master" Lucas, but which is now in the hands of a new generation of heroes.

"The Snores Awaken" certainly won't be the last of *MAD*'s *Star Wars* parodies (there's another one in the next issue), and *MAD* won't stop spoofing the saga any time soon. "It's a really rich universe," says Bresman. "So there's any number of angles you can mine it for. I think that's why *Star Wars* is unique, and why it feeds into *MAD* so well. Not just from a story perspective, but also visually. There's so much for *MAD* to work with!"

It's safe to say that the Farce will be with us, always... ☸

Arie Kaplan is an author and comedy writer who has written more than two dozen articles for MAD *magazine (three of which were* Star Wars *parodies). He has written two* LEGO Star Wars *books for Scholastic:* Face Off *(published September 2016) and* The Official Stormtrooper Training Manual *(coming January 2017). Visit his website at ariekaplan.com and follow him on Twitter @ariekaplan.*

┌ **MORE TO SAY**
MAD About Star Wars, edited by Jonathan Bresmen is available now.
HAVE YOU?

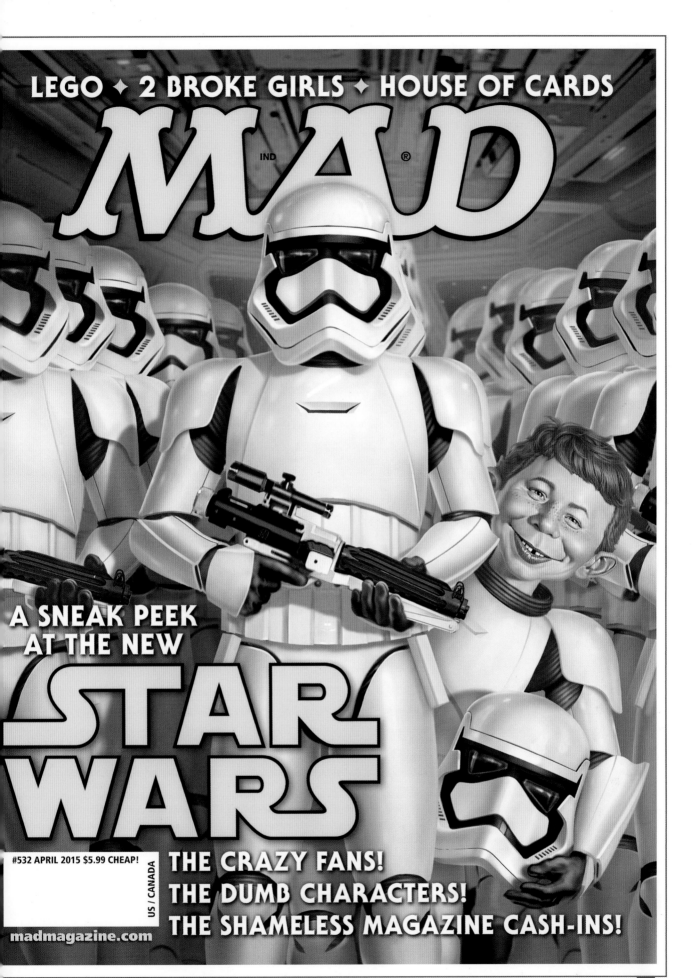

LEGO ✦ 2 BROKE GIRLS ✦ HOUSE OF CARDS

MAD

IND ®

A SNEAK PEEK
AT THE NEW

STAR
WARS

#532 APRIL 2015 $5.99 CHEAP!

US / CANADA

THE CRAZY FANS!
THE DUMB CHARACTERS!
THE SHAMELESS MAGAZINE CASH-INS!

madmagazine.com

STAR WARS WARS

INSIDER

EXCLUSIVE!
A NEW DAWN
Creating the Stunning
Rebels Prequel Novel!

DROID DESIGN!
Meet the Man who
Builds Real-life Droids!

ISSUE #152
US $7.99
CAN $9.99
OCTOBER 2014

TITAN

STAR WARS REBELS
MEET THE CREW OF THE *GHOST*!
THE REBELS: INTERVIEWED INSIDE!
SECRETS OF THE SHOW REVEALED!

TAYLOR GRAY
EZRA BRIDGER

ISSUE 152
OCTOBER 2014

Star Wars Rebels premieres with double-length first episode, *Spark of Rebellion*

William Shakespeare's Star Wars Trilogy: The Royal Imperial Box Set by Ian Doescher, published by Quirk Books

Star Wars: The Adventures of Luke Skywalker, Jedi Knight by Tony DiTerlizzi with concept art by Ralph McQuarrie, published by Disney Lucasfilm Press

Star Wars Costumes: The Original Trilogy by Brandon Alinger, with a foreword by John Mollo, published by Chronicle Books

Over three short years, *Star Wars Rebels*' Ezra Bridger has grown into one of the most intriguing characters in *Star Wars* lore. From Force-sensitive street urchin to an essential part of the *Ghost* crew, he has matured under the tutelage of Kanan Jarrus, but has shown a worrying penchant for harnessing the dark side.

This was *Insider*'s first interview with Taylor Gray, the actor who plays Ezra, and it shows the passion he has had for the character since day one. Conducted in the days before Ezra's path was known (to us, anyway!), Gray can't say too much, but shares his excitement at coming into the *Star Wars* world and drops a few hints about who Ezra is to him. It's fascinating to look back on now!—Jonathan Wilkins

Taylor Arthur Gray (born September 7, 1993) played Bucket in the Nickelodeon series Bucket & Skinner's Epic Adventures *and animator Friz Freleng in the movie* Walt Before Mickey *(2015). He played the lead alongside Kevin Durant in the 2012 basketball movie* Thunderstruck.

REBEL WITH

STAR WARS REBELS MARKS ACTOR TAYLOR GRAY'S FIRST TIME DOING VOICE-OVER WORK. HE TOLD *STAR WARS INSIDER* ABOUT HIS EXPERIENCES PLAYING THE FORCE-SENSITIVE KID OF THE GROUP, EZRA BRIDGER. INTERVIEW: AMY RATCLIFFE

Star Wars Insider: Tell us about Ezra Bridger and what you like about the character.

Taylor Gray: I have grown to like everything about this character. He's a young kid who is Force-sensitive, and he's unaware that he's tapping into something bigger than himself. He believes at first that these innate strange abilities are just instinctive and part of who he is, but once he comes across the rebel crew, the other characters begin to open up his eyes and teach him what powers he really has. He begins to harness them. It's very fun because he's not a bad kid, but he's a kid who's been wronged by the Empire. He's maybe a little sour about that and therefore acts on those feelings. I think he embodies the word "rebel" through and through.

Ezra is practically living on the streets and getting by on his own on the planet Lothal, but when he meets the crew of the *Ghost*, he's no longer alone. What's it like for him to basically gain a family?

It's hard for him at first. When he comes across the other rebels and they try to bring him in, at first, he's completely opposed to it. He wants to go back and handle things on his own, but he has a bond with Kanan and Kanan is the real reason why he stays with the rebel crew. Kanan went through the same type of things as Ezra did as far as being Force-sensitive, so he's able to connect with him on that level and their relationship grows. Theirs is one of the main relationships throughout the show. That's the real reason he stays, and he ends up enjoying having a family. It's something he hasn't had for a while so it means a lot to him, and he becomes very loyal and makes [the crew of the *Ghost*] his first priority.

As you got deeper into the story and saw what the Empire was like in this time period, what surprised you?

It's cool because *Rebels* bridges the gap between the two trilogies in the saga. I feel like that's a pretty big section of *Star Wars* that hasn't been tapped into, and I think that it's so cool to follow the rebels. They're the ones I was rooting on when I was younger; I always wanted the rebels to beat the Empire [in the original trilogy]. [In *Star Wars Rebels*] The Empire is in control of things, but there's hope—the show kind of hangs on that word. The rebels are starting to come up with some plans, and they're gaining some power and strength and beginning a movement. The rebels are leading that charge. They're the trailblazers.

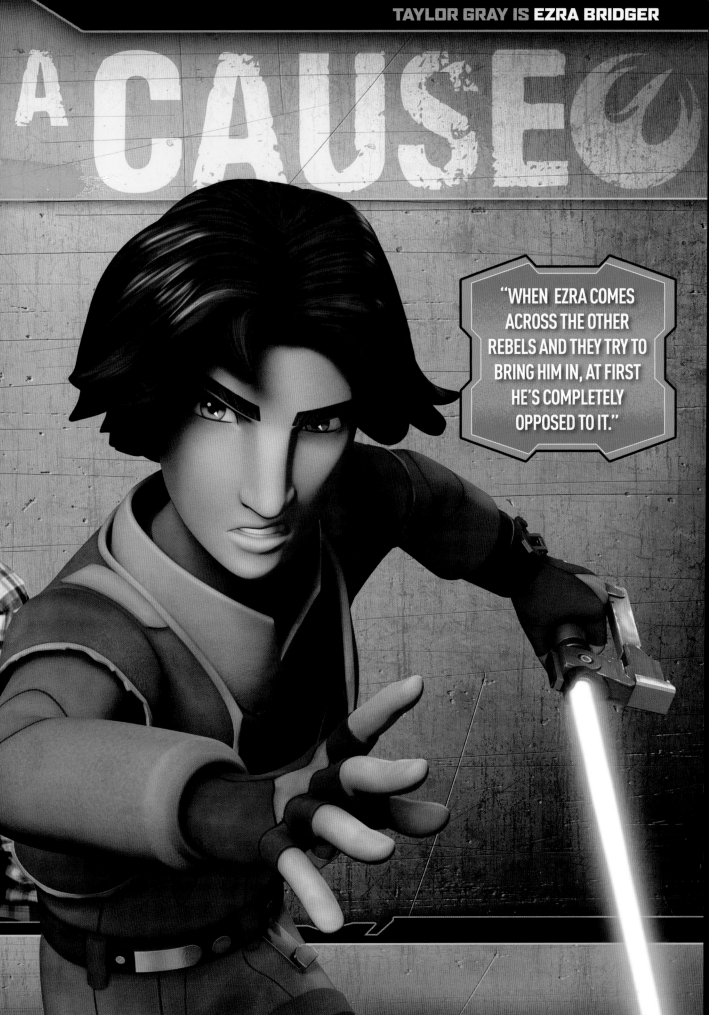

A CAUSE

"WHEN EZRA COMES ACROSS THE OTHER REBELS AND THEY TRY TO BRING HIM IN, AT FIRST HE'S COMPLETELY OPPOSED TO IT."

Star Wars Rebels features a ragtag sort of group fighting against the Empire, and it seems to parallel Episode IV. Do you see any similarities between them?

It's completely true. That little group they have [in Episode IV], that's what you feel on this show. I think what got everyone excited about the original *Star Wars* movies is that group's dynamic and the rapport between all of them. They all speak their mind, they're all opinionated and strong characters, and that's how the rebels are. There's definitely a parallel between the characters but also the storylines—it's still a group trying to fight against the Empire even though there are a lot of things and obstacles that get in the way.

> "WE GO DEEP INTO THESE CHARACTERS, WHICH I FEEL KIND OF LACKS SOMETIMES IN ANIMATION."

What are you most excited for fans to see in *Star Wars Rebels*?

The animation. That's something that I keep talking about. When I was at *Star Wars* Weekends I was mentioning to everyone that it blows my mind how good it is. I've seen little clips here and there, and the parts I have seen look unbelievable. People are going to be blown away. It references Ralph McQuarrie's original artwork for *Star Wars* and aesthetically, everything is beautiful.

Also, the dialogue of the show is awesome. It's like the original trilogy in the sense that it has that sarcastic, witty banter. The dialogue is so exciting, even without the action—don't get me wrong, there's a ton of action in *Rebels*—but the dialogue is so on point. We go deep into these characters, which I feel is sometimes lacking in animation. I think people are really going to have their favorites and relate to certain characters.

And the weapons that are used! Ezra has this slingshot with these little stun-type balls on his wrist, and I think that's a new thing that we haven't seen.

This is the first time you've done voice-acting work. What a group to start with! What's the transition to voice-acting been like, and what's it like in the recording room?

Oh, it's a blast. Everything has been different.

"[BEING A GUEST AT] *STAR WARS* WEEKENDS WAS THE COOLEST THING... PEOPLE ARE STOKED ABOUT *REBELS*!"

Normally there's a camera, you sit through an hour of hair and makeup, and you've got to block shots. This is amazing because I can walk in wearing sweats. It's so fun, and everyone is there. I guess that's not a normal thing with animation, but Dave Filoni, the head of it all, the mastermind, says he really likes that and I understand because it's easier to work off of people—it's really great for all of us. We've all become so close.

On the first day, I got so many notes! We go for a take and I would turn to Freddie Prinze Jr., who plays Kanan, and say my lines just as I normally would. He would glance at me, but then when he would say his lines he kept looking forward. And then at the end of the take, they'd say, "That was a great one, but can we just do it again and Taylor, can you make sure you look at the mic?" I'm like, "Oh yeah, of course." It took a little while to get used to that and to look at a little microphone in front of you rather than everyone else. Once I got used to that though, it just flowed.

You mentioned *Star Wars* Weekends. You appeared at two of them. What was it like to attend and already be like a rock star to fans before *Star Wars Rebels* has even aired?
It blew my mind. I had no idea what I was in store for. Going two weekends in a row was fun because the next weekend I got to bring my entire family out and I kind of knew the ropes a little bit more, and I was more comfortable. But that first weekend, it was literally insane. It was the coolest thing. So many people are looking forward to it [*Rebels*], which I did not expect. I thought maybe some people would come up and talk to me and know me from other things I've done but no, people are stoked about *Rebels*. It just got me even more excited because I got to talk about it for six days straight.

It's so cool to hear people's theories and what they think is going to happen. I've got to say some fans are spot-on, and I have to be like, "Oh, maybe that will happen," when in the back of my mind I'm like, "Wow, it's like you had one of our scripts!" It seems like there is a code of ethics for *Star Wars* fans in general because everyone was incredibly nice and incredibly passionate, but they all had respect and understood when I couldn't say anything. I felt so honored and grateful to be able to talk to them and meet so many awesome people. It was a blast for me and I just hope that we get to go to more of them because it was so fun.

There are already fans dressing like Ezra. Does that surprise you?
I think I took three or four pictures with different Ezras. It was insane. I feel like I keep repeating myself, but it blew my mind. I didn't expect that. I know they've only released a little bit of information so far about *Rebels*, but people are grabbing it and running with it. I just hope they enjoy the show as much as we enjoy making it. I think it's really something of quality. ☻

REBELS *ROGUE ONE* COLLECTOR'S COVER
CHOOSE YOUR SIDE: ARE YOU WITH THE REBELS OR THE EMPIRE

STAR WARS
INSIDER

THE OFFICIAL MAGAZINE OF THE *STAR WARS* SAGA

FEATURING THE STARS OF *ROGUE ONE*!

THE VOICE OF THE EMPIRE

Read an exclusive
Star Wars story,
only in this issue!

ISSUE #170
US $7.99
CAN $9.99
JAN/FEB 2017

TITAN

MEET THE REBELS ON A MISSION...
ROGUE ONE

DONNIE YEN AND JIANG WEN
GUARDIANS OF THE WHILLS

ISSUE 170
JAN/FEB 2017

Star Wars: Han Solo trade paperback by Marjorie Liu and Mark Brooks, published by Marvel Comics (January))

Star Wars: Darth Maul, Part 1 by Cullen Bunn with art by Luke Ross, published by Marvel Comics (February)

Star Wars Aftermath: Empire's End by Chuck Wendig, published by Del Rey (February)

Star Wars Legends Epic Collection: The Newspaper Strips: Volume 1, published by Marvel Comics (February)

Rogue One: A Star Wars Story is a movie blessed with many scene-stealing turns. But for me the highlight was probably Donnie Yen and Jiang Wen as Chirrut Îmwe and Baze Malbus, who deserve to join the rich pantheon of *Star Wars* double acts alongside C-3PO and R2-D2, and Han Solo and Chewbacca.

The two actors play off each other brilliantly over the course of the movie, with Chirrut's belief in the Force and mastery of martial arts a sharp contrast to Baze's skepticism and skill with heavy artillery. It's a real shame that the events of the movie preclude the pair from having any more on-screen adventures.—**Jonathan Wilkins**

Donnie Yen *(born July 27, 1963), also known as* **Yen Ji-dan** *(甄子丹), is one of Hong Kong's top action stars. He is credited for bringing mixed martial arts into mainstream Chinese culture by featuring it in many of his movies.*
Jiang Wen *(born January 5, 1963) is an actor, writer, and director. He starred in the acclaimed director Zhang Yimou's debut film* Red Sorghum *(1987), and co-wrote, directed, and starred in the multi-award-winning* Devils on the Doorstep *(2000).*

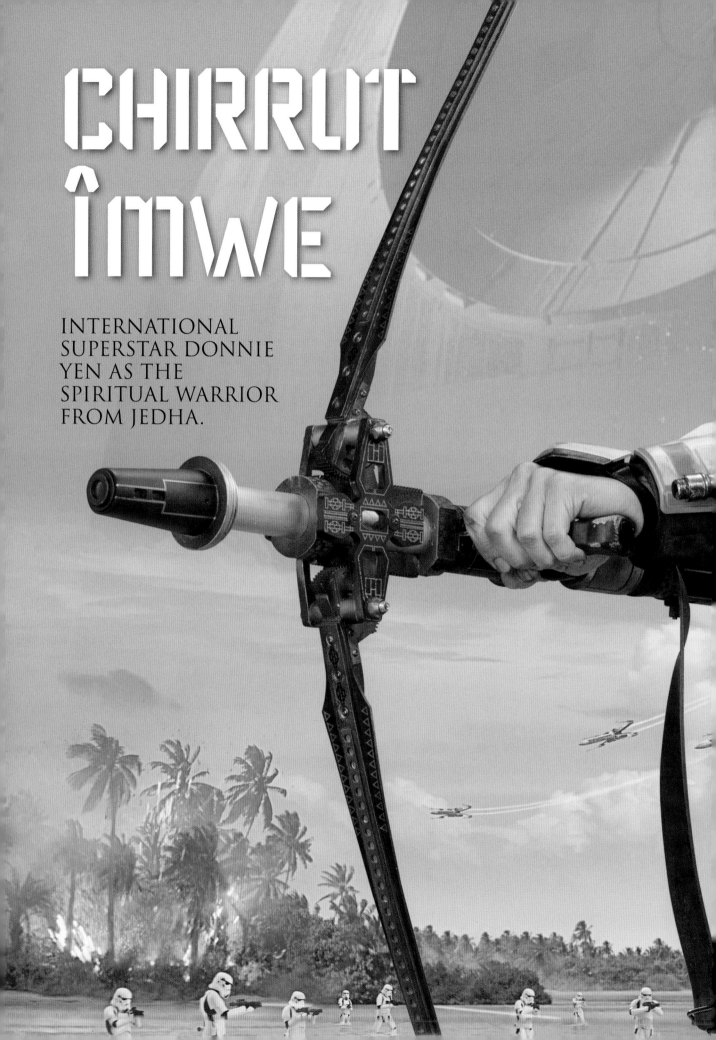

CHIRRUT ÎMWE

INTERNATIONAL
SUPERSTAR DONNIE
YEN AS THE
SPIRITUAL WARRIOR
FROM JEDHA.

For Donnie Yen, *Star Wars* is a family affair. With a little help from Disney, who provided the fabric, and the Bullet Films costume design team in Hong Kong, Yen's son James dressed up as his character, the blind warrior Chirrut Îmwe, for Halloween. Not to be outdone, Yen's daughter Jasmine cosplayed as a stormtrooper, with Yen proudly sharing a picture on Instagram. Chirrut may not have Force abilities in the movie, but no doubt the Force is with Yen and his family.

Born in Guangzhou, China, Yen moved to Hong Kong as a child and then to Boston when he was 11. His mother is a grandmaster in Fu Style Wudang Quan and Tai Chi, and Yen also studied many other forms of martial arts, including Karate, boxing, and Taekwondo. In the 2008 international box office smash *Ip Man*, Yen starred as the Wing Chun grandmaster Yip Man, famed as the instructor of the legendary martial artist and actor Bruce Lee. The movie's success and Yen's performance have been credited for the rise in popularity of Wing Chun in the years since its release. Yen is not just a martial artist however. He is also a pianist and breakdancer.

Yen first broke into the film industry in 1984 when he earned the leading role in *Drunken Tai Chi*. Following *Tiger Cage* (1988), he played Commander Lan in *Once Upon a Time in China II* (1992), starring another martial arts legend, Jet Li. Yen and Li appeared together again in the film *Hero*, which was nominated for Best Foreign Language Film at the 2003 Academy Awards. After playing Chen Zhen in the television series *Fist of Fury* (1995), Yen reprised the role in *Legend of the Fist: The Return of Chen Zhen* (2010).

For those not familiar with Yen's foreign roles, you may recognize him from the U.S. releases of *Highlander: Endgame* (2000) and *Blade II* (2002), where he had brief cameo roles. In a more substantial role, Yen played the villain Wu Chan in *Shanghai Knights* (2003), opposite Jackie Chan and Owen Wilson. And when he's not acting in front of the camera, Yen is often invited by Hollywood to choreograph action sequences, like he did for the espionage thriller *Stormbreaker* (2006). He's even been known to lend his martial-art skill to videogames as he choreographed the fight animations for Onimusha 3 (2004). And if that still isn't enough, Yen founded Bullet Films, where he produced and directed *Legend of the Wolf* (1997), and then produced *Ballistic Kiss* (1998).

While expanding his global presence, Yen has continued to take leading roles in Hong Kong cinema, including the wuxia epic film *Seven Swords* and the crime drama film *SPL: Kill Zone*, both featured at the 2005 Toronto International Film Festival. Yen acted

in, produced, and choreographed *Flash Point* (2007), for which he won the award for Best Action Choreography at the Golden Horse Film Awards and an acting award at the Hong Kong Film Awards. Not limiting himself to action roles, Yen appeared in the romantic comedy series *All's Well, Ends Well* in 2011 and 2012.

Yen has also used his success to support charities. In 2015, he brought donations and gifts to refugee camps in Thailand. He is also an ambassador for the international charity Free the Children. After winning a defamation lawsuit, he founded Yen's Honour Protection Fund, to empower celebrities to defend their

reputations from libelous falsehoods using available legal remedies.

For *Rogue One*, Yen brings to the table not only the diversity of his heritage and acting background, but also his commitment to playing the first major *Star Wars* film character with a physical disability. Chirrut Îmwe is a staff-wielding spiritual warrior who is also blind. At the *Rogue One* panel at Celebration Europe, Yen shared his take on his character: "Chirrut can't see, but he can feel with his heart and believes in the Force." As the trailers demonstrate, Chirrut's blindness is no impediment to his heroism against the Empire. ☻

"CHIRRUT CAN'T SEE, BUT HE CAN FEEL WITH HIS HEART AND BELIEVES IN THE FORCE."

Chirrut Îmwe faces a stormtrooper squad on Jedha.

Chirrut Îmwe (Donnie Yen) meets Jyn Erso (Felicity Jones).

Chirrut and Baze Malbus (Jiang Wen) after a fight.

BAZE MALBUS

THE ACCLAIMED
ACTOR, WRITER
AND DIRECTOR
JIANG WEN
TAKES AIM AS A
GUN-TOTING
WARRIOR WITH
A MISSION!

Baze Malbus (Jiang Wen) and Chirrut Îmwe (Donnie Yen): key players in the fight against the Empire!

"BAZE MALBUS IS A PRAGMATIST WHO—LIKE HAN SOLO— PREFERS A GOOD BLASTER AT HIS SIDE."

Baze Malbus made an unforgettable first impression in the trailer for *Rogue One*: standing in front of a downed X-wing, heavily armed and clad in red armor while blasting stormtroopers. He may be the muscle in the fight against the Empire, but don't let that fool you. The renowned Chinese actor who plays him, Jiang Wen, is also an internationally respected screenwriter and director, with a career reaching back to the early 1980s. *Devils on the Doorstep*, a black comedy he co-wrote and directed, won second place in the 2000 Cannes Film Festival Grand Prix, and as a result of that movie, *TIME Asia* has described him as a real-life rebel.

A graduate of the Central Academy of Drama, China's premier acting school, Jiang's breakout role in his home country came in the award-winning *Hibiscus Town* (1986), a chronicle of one woman's life

during China's Cultural Revolution. Though he has mostly worked on the big screen, his rise to fame really took off with a role in the television show *A Native of Beijing in New York* in the early 1990s. Around the same time he wrote and directed his first movie, *In The Heat Of The Sun* (1994), praised by *Variety* for its well-observed characters.

Shot in black and white, *Devils on the Doorstep* (2000) was only the second movie Jiang directed, and initially ran to three hours. Conventional wisdom suggested it could not succeed: not only because of its length and styling, but also because it was set against the backdrop of the Second Sino-Japanese War, causing discomfort for both the Chinese Film Board and his Japanese producers, who tried to curb Jiang's vision. However, the finished film was met with acclaim, and Jiang's uncompromising vision in the face of

doubters might remind western moviegoers of some of America's best-known cinematic rebels, such as George Lucas and James Cameron.

As the 21st century got underway, Jiang starred in a string of Chinese movies before a return to writing and directing with the romantic fantasy *The Sun Also Rises* (2007). In 2009 he was one of 11 directors to contribute to the anthology movie *New York, I Love You*, along with Natalie Portman and Mira Nair (*Queen of Katwe*). For his segment of the film, Jiang directed Hayden Christensen. He then went on to write, direct, and act in *Let the Bullets Fly* (2010), an action comedy that became China's highest grossing domestic

Baze in the heat of battle on the war-torn streets of Jedha.

film ever, holding the record for two years.

At London's Celebration Europe in summer 2016, fans got their first hints about the character of Baze Malbus and his camaraderie with Chirrut Îmwe—whom he is defending in that memorable trailer clip. While Îmwe, played by legendary Hong Kong martial arts actor Donnie Yen, is deeply spiritual and a believer in the Force, Malbus is a pragmatist who—like Han Solo—prefers a good blaster at his side, backed up with a healthy dose of bravado. Asked for a description of his character, Jiang answered, "Baze has a gun. He has a huge gun." When the Empire comes calling on the planet Jedha, you can be sure he's going to use it! ☮

A former Guardian of the Whills, Baze has rejected his faith.

ANTHONY DANIELS ON THE PERILS OF PLAYING C-3PO!

STAR WARS
INSIDER

REVENGE OF THE SITH!

We Celebrate the 10th
Anniversary of Episode III

ISSUE #157
US $7.99
CAN $9.99
MAY/JUNE 2015

TITAN

LORDS OF MISRULE

The Emperor and Darth Vader unite in an all-new tale—inside!

EXPLORING THE LIGHTER SIDE!

Jeffrey Brown on Finding
Good in Darth Vader!

DARK EMPIRE
DARK HORSE COMICS

ISSUE 157
MAY/JUNE 2015

Star Wars Rebels: Always Bet on Chopper by Meredith Rusu released as part of the Disney Lucasfilm Press World of Reading series (May)

Star Wars Legends Epic Collection: *The New Republic* Volume 1 published by Marvel Comics (May)

Christopher Lee, Count Dooku in *Attack of the Clones* and *Revenge of the Sith* passes away on June 7

Jeffrey Brown's *Star Wars Jedi Academy: The Phantom Bully* published by Scholastic (June)

In 2015, writer Tom Veitch and illustrator Cam Kennedy's epic 1980s comic-book *The Light and Darkness War* was reprinted, giving *Insider* an excuse to look back at the duo's much-loved *Star Wars* series, *Dark Empire*. Originally released by Dark Horse Comics between December 1991 and October 1992 as a six-issue bi-monthly series, the acclaimed series was followed by two sequels: *Dark Empire II* and *Empire's End*.

Originally presented in two parts, Michael Kogge's in-depth appreciation features rare bonus material, including detailed notes that shed light on the artistic choices that go into creating such a fondly remembered masterpiece.—**Jonathan Wilkins**

Tom Veitch (born September 26, 1951) started out as a contributor to the influential underground comix movement of the early 1970s. His best-known work includes Star Wars: Dark Empire *and* Tales of the Jedi; *a run on* Animal Man *for DC Comics; and two* Elseworlds *series featuring Kamandi and an elder Superman, also for DC.*
Cam Kennedy (born October 15, 1944) began his comics career in his native Scotland working on British war comic Commando *for D.C. Thomson. He is best known for his work on* 2000AD, *contributing to the early success of characters such as Judge Dredd. His* Star Wars *work aside from* Dark Empire *includes several Boba Fett one-shots.*

OF REBEL DREAMS AND
DARK EMPIRES
THE MAKING OF A *STAR WARS* LEGEND

BY MICHAEL KOGGE

STAR WARS INSIDER REVEALS HOW WRITER TOM VEITCH AND ARTIST CAM KENNEDY CONTINUED THE STAR WARS SAGA WHEN ALL HOPE SEEMED LOST.

Left: Dave Dorman's evocative cover art for *Dark Empire* signaled the triumphant return of *Star Wars* to comic stores, but few could have predicted the myriad twists and turns that the saga would take.

By 1988, *Star Wars* had faded from the limelight of mainstream popular culture. *Return of the Jedi* had finished its theatrical run five years before, and, though rumors persisted, there seemed to be no future films on the horizon. The only new *Star Wars* material being produced was Blackthorne's *Star Wars 3-D* comics and role-playing adventures published by a small Pennsylvania company, West End Games. For most of the public, *Star Wars* had become just another tape to rent at the local video store.

That was never the case for writer Tom Veitch.

When the curtains closed on *Jedi*, Veitch didn't view it as the end of the *Star Wars* saga—he saw it as the beginning of a new era. George Lucas's rich universe now lay ripe for other storytellers to weave their own tales. Veitch dreamed up sequels and prequels, epics concerning the Clone Wars, the Sith, the Jedi, and Luke Skywalker's further adventures—the "before and after" of the *Star Wars* trilogy. But these stories didn't need to be told as expensive blockbuster films. Veitch believed the medium best suited for continuing the saga was the one he'd been writing for since boyhood, which was also the medium that had inspired Lucas to make *Star Wars*: Comics.

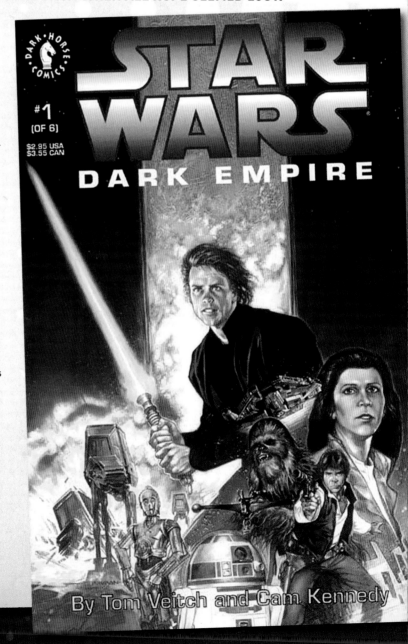

DARK HORSE COMICS

STAR WARS

#1 (OF 6)

$2.95 USA
$3.55 CAN

DARK EMPIRE

By Tom Veitch and Cam Kennedy

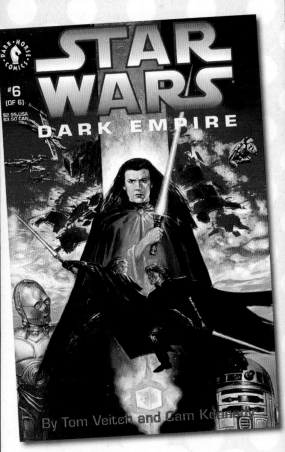

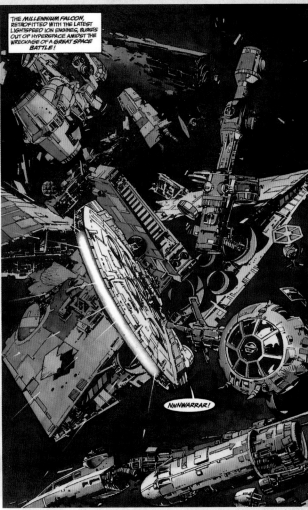

THE *MILLENNIUM FALCON*, RETROFITTED WITH THE LATEST LIGHTSPEED ION ENGINES, BURSTS OUT OF HYPERSPACE AMIDST THE WRECKAGE OF A *GREAT SPACE BATTLE!*

NNNWARRAR!

Far left: Issue number #6 showed something fans had speculated about for a long time: Leia brandishing a lightsaber.

Left: A typically spectacular panel by Cam Kennedy showing the aftermath of a battle.

A PROPOSAL

On November 19, 1988, after discussions with Scottish artist Cam Kennedy, Veitch wrote a short letter to filmmaker George Lucas proposing a new *Star Wars* comic book series. It would be rendered in the same fully-painted style of *The Light and Darkness War*, the limited series from Marvel Epic that Veitch and Kennedy had created, and he offered to send samples.

Years of experience in publishing taught Veitch not to expect a reply. Most likely his letter would be tossed in a slush pile, discarded, unopened, or even returned as unsolicited. Still, he sent the letter. It was his message in the bottle, his hologram to Obi-Wan, his hope that the stories he'd been imagining for years would finally bear fruit.

"A curious thing happened as I was on the way to the post office to mail this letter," Veitch recalls. "It was an unusually warm day, and I walked by a house with its front windows open, out of which, at high volume, was pouring the John Williams soundtrack for *Star Wars*!" Three days later he received a phone call from Lucy Wilson, director of publishing at Lucasfilm. She said Lucasfilm was interested in the proposal, pending George Lucas's approval after seeing Veitch's samples. The next day Veitch sent off the first three issues of *The Light and Darkness War*. On November 29, he received a follow-up phone call from Wilson: Lucas had given his blessing and the project was a go.

In a matter of days, Veitch's musings on the Jedi suddenly seemed anything but dreams. He excitedly phoned Cam Kennedy in Scotland and the two dared themselves to create the most cinematic comic they could on paper. By December 2, Veitch had dashed off a concept idea for what he tentatively titled The Jedi Chronicles.

Getting official permission actually proved to be the easiest step in an arduous three-year journey that nearly saw the comic terminated more than once. Despite the pitfalls, Veitch and Kennedy's tenacity to bring their project to fruition resulted in a series that changed the comics industry just as *Star Wars* changed films.

This is the saga of *Dark Empire*.

TOM'S STORY

Thomas Veitch grew up in the Golden Age of comic books. While an issue nowadays costs nearly five dollars, in the 1940s and '50s they were only a dime. Veitch and his three younger brothers were able to spend their allowances at the local drugstores in New Hampshire and Vermont, collecting and reading every comic book they could get their hands on.

"We weren't allowed to read horror and crime comics, but fortunately the neighbors, who lived in a one-room shack without plumbing, had all the forbidden titles, and we sat around their smelly house reading them," Veitch says.

Artistic talent ran in the family. Before he met his wife, Veitch's father had passed the Disney drawing test and had considered moving from Vermont to California to work in animation. Though he took up a factory job to support his growing family, all four of his sons shared his interest in drawing, with young Tom leading the way.

"I started a 'publishing company' that produced numerous hand-drawn comic book titles, in editions of one copy each," he remembers fondly. "My favorite was a space epic I wrote and drew that ran 20 or 30 issues. I was influenced by *Buck Rogers*, *Flash Gordon*, *Tom Corbet Space Cadet*, and the EC science-fiction comic books. And then there was my one-shot take on *Archie* comics, in which the characters were laboriously copied from the original comics, except Betty and Veronica were drawn in every panel without any clothes on!

"I was probably a better figure artist as a kid than I am now. That's because my brother Rick came along and he was very, very good. The rest of us stepped aside and let Rick be 'the cartoonist' of the family. I wrote and published the stories, and Rick drew them," Veitch says of his younger brother, who became a comics legend in his own right.

When the Comics Code Authority of 1954 began to censor comics, Veitch quickly

bored of the bland, predictable stories. Yet his eye caught the marvelous covers of the science-fiction paperbacks that were often sold in the same drugstore rack as comics. Soon he was devouring the futuristic tales of Arthur C. Clarke, Ray Bradbury, Poul Anderson, Clifford D. Simak, and A.E. van Vogt, among many others, while his interest in comics waned.

"The Code took the fire out of the writing, and even the art," Veitch says, "that is, until Stan Lee, Jack Kirby, Steve

Ditko and the Marvel gang tore up the town in the 1960s. We were all nuts for Kirby's new style—clearly, he had crossed a threshold and tapped into the imagination in a way nobody else had. My brother Rick and I painted a huge panorama of the Marvel characters on Rick's bedroom wall, dominated by Galactus, his hand reaching out at you, fingers curled in that unique way Kirby used to draw gloved fingers."

Veitch spent two years at Columbia

University in New York, until unfortunate unforeseen medical circumstances forced him to return home. "I had to go into seclusion for about a year, working as a garage mechanic in Vermont, until I recovered'"

After recovery, he lived the very bohemian life of a poet in New York's Lower East Side until something radical happened. "I began having out-of-body experiences, much like my character Laz in *The Light and Darkness War*. Except, unlike Laz, I didn't travel to warrior's Valhalla—I was fortunate to get a tour of the more pleasant dimensions.

"I know now that all of these 'alternate realities' are part of the psyche. They're just unconscious to us most of the time, as long as our focus is on day-to-day survival in the world. But back then, in the mid-1960s, they were religious experiences to me, and I ended up going into a monastery for two-and-a-half years."

In January 1968, Veitch left the quiet chambers of the Benedictine monastery for a counterculture of another kind. In San Francisco, months after the "Summer of Love," Veitch found a place true to all his passions. He met his wife-to-be, published underground "comix" with artist Greg Irons, wrote wordplay novels in the vein of the Beat writers, and befriended literary luminaries such as Allen Ginsberg. Ginsberg even featured Veitch as a character in one of his poems and later contributed an afterword to a 1976 collected edition of Veitch's own poetry.

The underground comix movement died out as conservatism took hold of American politics, but Veitch's passion for comics did not. In the 1980s, after becoming a bookseller and poetry teacher, Veitch turned his sights toward reaching a broader audience. Success arrived in his collaboration with artist Cam Kennedy.

Left: *Star Wars* on an epic scale! Veitch and Kennedy's story featured imagery fans of the saga had never seen before.

ALLEN GINSBERG FEATURED VEITCH AS A CHARACTER IN ONE OF HIS POEMS.

CAM'S STORY

Alexander Campbell ("Cam") Kennedy began drawing at the wee age of two-and-a-half—at least according to his mother, who encouraged her son's talent. Born a "war baby" as the conflict against Hitler neared its end, Kennedy was raised in Glasgow, Scotland, where it was unusual for someone to become a professional artist. Sons were expected to follow their fathers into the dockyards or shipbuilding companies. But Kennedy refused to train as an engineer like his father. When he turned 16, he rebelled against everybody—even his mother—and left school to work in a commercial art studio.

"My mother was still waiting for me when I was in my 40s to get a proper job. She felt this was just a whim, being an artist," Kennedy says, with a laugh. "She changed her mind when one of the TV channels in Britain did a documentary about comic-strip artists. Then, of course, I was her blue-eyed boy because she could mention to her friends at the post office, 'Did you see my son on the television last night?' Typical mom, you know."

In 1962, Kennedy left Scotland and went down to London, which had started to swing with an energy of its own. The Beatles were on the brink of mass popularity, along with other bands such as the Rolling Stones, who lived on the next street over from Kennedy. "There was a huge mass of talent coming from all over Britain," Kennedy remembers, "writers, musicians, artists, everything. It was a great time to be there, absolutely wonderful."

Kennedy's wanderlust pulled him across the English Channel to hitchhike around Europe, then to Normandy, France. A local family took him in as one of their own. "The original story was I was going to draw the old church in the town. But the family joke was that that was in 1965 and I still haven't drawn the church!"

Kennedy learned the language and made his living selling oil paintings and wedding portraits from a room in the family's house. "People stopped to come in and ask if they could see what the painter was doing. The great thing about being foreign in these countries is you're a big draw, because people are quite taken with the accent you have," Kennedy says. "They just wanted to see what a Northern Scotsman looked liked."

When Kennedy returned to Scotland in 1966 with his "little French wife," a friend recommended that he should draw comics for publisher D.C. Thomson & Co. Though Kennedy's interests at the time were in fine art and folk music, he had read comics when he was younger and thought it might be fun to have a go at it. So he made some illustrations of soldiers and sent them to the editor at D.C. Thomson. "The guy phoned me the next day and said, 'Can you come to the head office and we'll give you a script.' I said, 'Oh, that was easy!'"

For the next six years, Kennedy drew for D.C. Thomson's famous *Commando* war comic, then went to work as a fine artist and watercolorist in Normandy. He returned to comics in the late 1970s, penciling and inking the *Battle* comic magazine strip "Fighting Mann" for Fleetway Publications in London, transitioning over to their weekly science-fiction anthology, *2000 A.D.*, where he drew *Rogue Trooper* and later the *Judge Dredd* comic, collaborating with writers and fellow Scotsmen John Wagner and Alan Grant.

At one point, he was working through the night, fueled by whiskey and BBC radio, producing six pages of *Dredd* and three-to-four pages of *Trooper* a week. "It was one of those periods where you have got a real flow on—it just flows out continually," Kennedy says. "After that I got into doing things like *Light and Darkness* and then eventually *Dark Empire*."

Above: An excerpt from the initial proposal for *Dark Empire*, then called "The Jedi Chronicles."

Right: Kennedy and Veitch's *The Light and Darkness War* was instrumental in convincing Lucasfilm —and George Lucas himself—that the time was right for *Star Wars* to continue as a comic book.

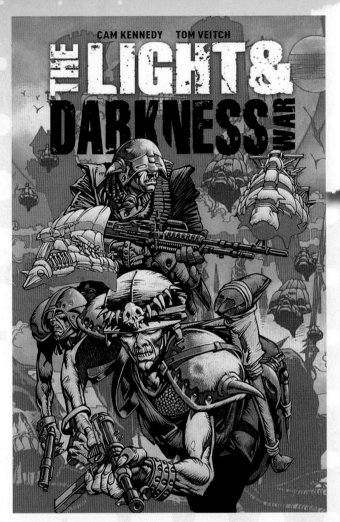

WHEN CAM MET TOM (THROUGH STEVE)

In the early 1980s, Steve Bissette, an American artist who worked with *Watchmen* writer Alan Moore on DC Comics' *Saga of the Swamp Thing*, was in London for a convention that Kennedy also attended. The two got on really well and Kennedy traveled to the States to visit Bissette at his home in Vermont. Bissette invited his writer-friend Tom Veitch over for dinner one evening, and Veitch and Kennedy started discussing future projects they had in mind. "That time I was really looking for something to do with warriors," Kennedy recalls.

As fortune would have it, Veitch was mulling over a similar idea he was planning to pitch to Marvel Epic editor Archie Goodwin. "Cam told me about a recurring image he had, of an ancient warrior on a strange beast, looking up at the sky as a World War II fighter plane breaks through the clouds. 'I'm thinking of a time-travel story,' he said. I pulled a four-page treatment for *The Light and Darkness War* out of my pocket—a tale of the coming together of warriors and technology from different eras—and that was it."

Little did either of them know, *The Light and Darkness War* would plant the seeds of a second collaboration, *Star Wars: Dark Empire*, which would become one of the best-selling comics of the 1990s, and would carve their names in both *Star Wars* lore and comics history.

OF LIGHT AND DARKNESS

THE MAKING OF *DARK EMPIRE* – PART II

BY MICHAEL KOGGE

INSIDER CONTINUES ITS LOOK BACK AT THE ICONIC COMIC SERIES FROM THE EARLY 1990S.

Right: Dave Dorman's iconic cover art for issue #2 showed a darker side to Luke Skywalker.

Opposite Page: Limited edition prints showcasing Cam Kennedy's stunning art.

Dark Empire is beloved by *Star Wars* fans as the comic book epic that tells how Luke Skywalker followed in his father's footsteps and turned, for a brief but galaxy-shaking moment, to the dark side of the Force. But what few fans know is that when writer Tom Veitch and Scottish artist Cam Kennedy first pitched their idea to Lucasfilm, it was for a prequel to the original trilogy, not a sequel. Veitch called it *The Jedi Chronicles*.

"Our first ambition is to examine the period between the first and second trilogies, when Darth Vader rose to preeminence as 'Dark Lord of the Sith.' We are told that it was during this 20 year span following the Clone Wars that Vader, 'hunted down and exterminated the remaining Jedi'—all except Yoda and Obi-Wan Kenobi," Veitch wrote in his proposal of December 2, 1988. "We would want to focus on the greatness of the martyred Masters, their wise and ingenious use of the Force, their awesome exploits against the Empire, and ultimately, their heroic deaths. Our book would end on an upbeat note, with Obi-Wan Kenobi watching young Luke Skywalker from afar, prophesying Luke's role in the struggle and victories yet to come."

Lucasfilm's director of publishing at that time, Lucy Wilson, rejected Veitch's proposal on the grounds that it might interfere with a prequel film trilogy George Lucas was considering making. She suggested an alternative timeline—why not *continue* the adventures of Luke Skywalker, after the events of *Return of the Jedi*? This would give Veitch and Kennedy carte blanche to do what they wanted, without worrying about contradicting future films. The two agreed on Wilson's timeline and commenced work on what would be the first sequel to the original film trilogy—in any form—since the days of the Marvel *Star Wars* comic, and a full year before author Timothy Zahn signed a contract to write his *Heir to the Empire* novel.

For Veitch, this was a dream project. He'd been a big fan of *Star Wars* since the 1970s, and often found himself imagining his own "tales of the Jedi" long after *Return of the Jedi* had left theaters. Veitch also realized this would be a difficult and demanding project, one which would require much thought and preparation to do it right. Though he had written underground comix and avant-garde novels in the 1970s, *Star Wars* delivered a different—and potentially much bigger—audience than his previous readership.

And while the galaxy of far, far away might have faded from mainstream popular culture, it still remained *the* galaxy of far, far away. No space fantasy film had eclipsed the success of the *Star Wars* trilogy, and its oft-quoted salutation— "May the Force be with you"—was forever part of American culture.

The Force would most definitely need to be with Veitch for his dream project to come to completion through the struggles that ensued.

THE LIGHT AND DARKNESS WAR

Reflecting on the origins of *Dark Empire*, it seems astonishing that Lucasfilm would hand over the keys to the *Star Wars* universe to a writer and artist who weren't yet household names among comic book fans in America. Although Kennedy had an enormous résumé across the pond in British comics, the most popular title he'd drawn was *Judge Dredd*, which was barely known in the States. Veitch had achieved success in bohemian circles and the San Francisco underground comix scene, but he supported his family by selling

antiquarian books and teaching the works of Carl Jung.

What connected both of these men— and perhaps what convinced Lucasfilm— was a passion for visual storytelling that wasn't beholden to current industry standards. Both men were rebels of sorts—Veitch the iconoclastic poet, Kennedy the wanderlust painter, each of who endeavored to break new ground in their creative work, despite commercial demands. Yet with Kennedy located in Scotland, and Veitch in Vermont, their collaboration—and thus *Dark Empire*— never would have happened if not for mutual friend and comic book veteran, Steve Bissette.

In the mid-1980s, Kennedy visited Bissette in Vermont and told him of an image he couldn't get out of his mind. He'd done a couple drawings, but was looking for a writer to help develop the idea. "It was of a Second World War bomber coming back from a raid over Germany and it goes through a timewarp, and then it finds itself on a parallel warrior plain somewhere on Earth," Kennedy says. "It's a weapon these warriors fighting below on the plain have never seen before."

Bissette told Kennedy he knew someone who could be a good collaborator and invited writer pal Tom Veitch over

YOU HAVE FILLED THE *GALAXY* WITH YOUR *DARKNESS* ... BUT I HAVE SEEN WHAT MY FATHER COULD NOT SEE...

I HAVE SEEN THAT ULTIMATELY THE DARK SIDE WILL *FAIL!*

JEDI FOOL... IN SPITE OF THE *STORIES* YOU TELL YOURSELF, *I* AM THE STRONGER... DID I NOT *WARN* YOU?

From top, this page: Luke takes on the cloned Emperor; the Empire's impressive battleship, the *Eclipse*; Kennedy's art conveys a strong sense of movement, bringing the climactic lightsaber duel to life.

Opposite page, from left: A shocking image from *Dark Empire* as Luke kneels before the Emperor; *The Light and Darkness War*'s Lazarus Jones proved to be an influential protagonist.

for dinner one evening. The two clicked instantly, and when Kennedy mentioned his idea, Veitch showed him a treatment for a similar multi-dimensional war story he'd been developing for several years. This serendipity resulted in what would be one of the most well-regarded comic book series of the 1980s, *The Light and Darkness War*. Epic Comics, a creator-owned imprint at Marvel under the supervision of editor Archie Goodwin, published the six issue series written by Veitch and illustrated by Kennedy, to great acclaim. The series was no wham-pow superhero saga, but a moving story about a crippled veteran of the Vietnam war, Lazarus Jones, who is transported into another universe and finds a new life leading a war against the evil Lord Na and his Deadsiders.

"Where did I get the idea for *The Light and Darkness War*? Frankly, it came out of my 'religious experiences' of years earlier, but also from reading Jung and learning his method of exploring the unconscious psyche. He was a very, very smart man—another Obi-Wan to me!" Veitch says. "Speaking of which, in those days everybody had been taken over by the *Star Wars*

NOW TAKE THE CONSEQUENCES OF *YOUR* FAILURE -- LIKE YOUR FATHER BEFORE YOU!

movies. So my imagination said to me, 'We can invent our own science-fiction universe, where there is good and evil, technology, war, and interesting characters —a big landscape of the imagination where just about anything we can think of can happen.'

"Vietnam came into it, because I was all too aware that thousands of men of my generation had gone there and died. The Vietnam Memorial—with its 50,000 names—had opened in 1982. Oliver Stone's film *Platoon* had been released in 1986, shortly before I met Cam. I had been hung up on the war for a long time, doing several comix stories about it with [legendary underground cartoonist] Greg Irons."

Readers familiar with *Dark Empire* will observe many parallels with *The Light and Darkness War*. Kennedy's trademark watercolor style is on full display, and many of the background characters in each series could be substituted without revision. The stories, too, share similar connections on the mythological level. "*Star Wars* has the Jedi, who are warrior-masters of the light. *The Light and Darkness War* has the Menteps, who are these curious aliens, not really human, who live in a kind of ongoing state of mystical rapport with 'the Source,' which is pure light and consciousness—equivalent to God, in Christian terms," Veitch says.

"*Star Wars* also has the Emperor, a Master of the dark side of the Force. We have Lord Na, who as a personality is nothing like the Emperor, but who is evil incarnate. He's also a kind of send-up of the Marvel super-villains. He's really stuck on himself, spouts arrogant bombast, and is surrounded by groveling sychophants—kind of like a modern politician!"

The influence of *The Light and Darkness War* reached well beyond Veitch and Kennedy's next project, *Dark Empire*. The term for Lord Na's undead minions, the "Deadsiders"— a word Veitch attributes to William Burroughs and Eric Frank Russell—has in turn been appropriated by television shows and role-playing games. Most notably, the series inspired director James Cameron to turn the hero of his blockbuster film *Avatar*, Jake Scully, into a paraplegic like Lazarus Jones.

FROM LAZARUS TO LUKE

After seeing the issues of *The Light and Darkness War* Veitch sent as samples, George Lucas—a comic book enthusiast—gave his blessing that Veitch and Kennedy could proceed with a *Star Wars* comic book series in Kennedy's fully painted style. Veitch ran with Wilson's advice that they go into the future rather than the past and quickly generated a new pitch. On the proposal's first page, Veitch put forward a bold request: that the villain of the comic

> THE SERIES INSPIRED DIRECTOR JAMES CAMERON TO TURN THE HERO OF HIS BLOCKBUSTER FILM *AVATAR*, JAKE SCULLY, INTO A PARAPLEGIC LIKE LAZARUS JONES.

book series should be the supreme Master of the dark side from the films, Emperor Palpatine.

Veitch posited many theories as to how the Emperor survived being flung into the Death Star's reactor, including one that he was not flesh-and-blood at all, but a machine. Perhaps most adventurous was imagining that the Emperor seen in the films was actually possessed by an evil alien intelligence. "This entity would probably come from outside the galaxy, and it would have a parasitical relationship to the Force," Veitch wrote at the time, and "its political subversion of the Republic (through the agency of Palpatine), would be part of a plan to transform the galaxy into a massive antheap society, with itself at the center. (The antheap image was suggested by the red-helmeted Imperial Guards, who made us think of red soldier ants.)"

But what best fit the story—and matched the reference to the "Clone

Wars" in *Star Wars*—was Veitch's idea that the Emperor found a way to survive by transferring his life force at the moment of annihilation into the bodies of younger clones. Palpatine's ultimate goal in the series would be to take possession of the body (and soul) of his arch-nemesis, the last of the Jedi, Luke Skywalker. This is the pitch Lucasfilm approved, and would tie in so well with the continuity of the prequels. In what might be the strongest link between the films and former "Expanded Universe" material developed by outside authors, George Lucas later used an iteration of this idea in *Revenge of the Sith*, when Darth Sidious reveals to Anakin Skywalker that if they work together, they could learn the dark side secret of subverting death.

THE RETURN OF ARCHIE GOODWIN

Veitch did not work alone in shaping the story of *Dark Empire*. Before he sent his proposal to Wilson, he bounced ideas off Kennedy and their *Light and Darkness* editor at Marvel Epic, Archie Goodwin, who had logged years exploring the *Star Wars* universe. In the late 1970s and early 1980s, Goodwin wrote the *Star Wars* daily syndicated comic for newspapers with artist Al Williamson, while also editing and writing more than 30 issues of Marvel's *Star Wars* monthly comic (see *Insider* 148 for a profile on Goodwin). No one in comics knew how to capture the spirit of *Star Wars* better than Goodwin, and it was for this reason that Veitch called Goodwin "Mr. *Star Wars*."

Working with Goodwin on *The Light and Darkness War* was, for Cam Kennedy, one of, "the highlights of my life." Editor and artist struck up a fast friendship, with Goodwin and his wife often hosting Kennedy in New York, and Goodwin visiting Kennedy at his home on a remote Scottish isle.

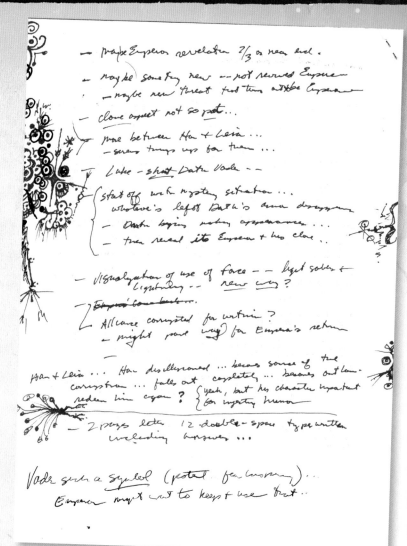

This page, from above: Tom Veitch's detailed notes; Veitch's script featured intriguing new information about the Jedi.

Opposite page, from left: A haunting image of Luke; one of Kennedy's spectacular battle scenes that would be recognized as one of the artist's many trademarks.

"He was very, very encouraging," Kennedy remembers of Goodwin. "When I drew out the first episode of *Light and Darkness*, he just liked it right away. He said, 'Keep firing off, this is great stuff, Cam.'"

Goodwin immediately warmed to Veitch and Kennedy's pitch for an adult, graphic novel version of *Star Wars* and said it would find a good home at Marvel Epic. Given this interest from a major publisher, on December 30, 1988, Veitch sent Goodwin his nine-page proposal and they batted it around, with Goodwin suggesting plot points of his own. "Archie came up with the idea that the Empire would put somebody else inside Vader's costume, to inspire fear throughout the galaxy," Veitch says.

With Goodwin's feedback, Veitch revised the proposal and sent it to Lucasfilm. Lucy Wilson approved Veitch to begin writing the scripts with one exception: "Anything to do directly with Vader was out. 'George is working on a prequel,'" Veitch recalls. "Meaning, I guess, that he didn't want us to contradict anything he might do with Vader in the prequels. She did say it was okay to use a 'training hologram' featuring Vader. And yes, it was okay to work from likenesses of the actors."

Veitch started writing, Kennedy started drawing, and all seemed well for *Star Wars* to make a

triumphant return in comics. Then in May 1989, Archie Goodwin left Marvel for a job at DC, and the new Epic editor didn't share Goodwin's enthusiasm for *Star Wars*. A year later, with the art for issue one completed, the publishing contracts still weren't finalized, and Veitch was doing all he could to keep Kennedy from moving onto other paying projects.

Dark Empire was suddenly in serious jeopardy.

DEATH TO THE DARK SIDE!

THE MAKING OF *DARK EMPIRE* – PART III

BY MICHAEL KOGGE

INSIDER CONCLUDES ITS LOOK BACK AT THE ICONIC COMIC SERIES FROM THE EARLY 1990S.

Right, from top:
Cam Kennedy's pencils become more fully-formed as Tom Veitch's dialogue is added by letterer Todd Klein.

In the beginning, there was the dark side and the light. Those on the side of good, the guardians of peace and justice in the galaxy, followed the light. Those who sought the heights of power or desired the galaxy for themselves, embraced the dark. Over 25 millennia, in a galaxy of long ago and far, far away, devotees of each battled in a seemingly eternal war of noble Jedi against evil Sith. If there was an intersection, it was most often when a soldier of the light was tempted and turned to the dark, only to meet an end in sorrow and despair. For as a wise Master once warned his young apprentice, "Once you start down the dark path, forever will it dominate your destiny."

In the mythological tradition of storytelling, warnings like these foreshadowed future conflicts. The genius of Tom Veitch and Cam Kennedy's *Dark Empire* was that they wove an entire epic comic series around that one line of dialogue. They turned that wise Master's young apprentice, Luke Skywalker, to the dark side.

And the dark side nearly won, taking the comic with it.

ARTIST IN JEOPARDY

By March 1990, Kennedy had completed all of his painted pages for issue one of *Dark Empire* based on Veitch's script. The plan called for Marvel Comics' Epic imprint to release the title because the story was more "adult" than the previous Marvel *Star Wars* series which had ended years before. But in the previous May, Archie Goodwin, the editor who had shepherded the

OH *GREAT!* THEY'RE BETWEEN US AND THE *FALCON!*

WHILE THE *WAR DROIDS* PIN US DOWN, THE *SCAVS* ARE GETTIN' OUT THEIR *TOOLS!*

project (and who was also one of the great *Star Wars* comics writers), departed Marvel for a move to DC. The new editors who replaced him didn't understand *Star Wars* like Goodwin did, and consequently failed to make *Dark Empire* a priority in Marvel's publishing program.

When contracts were not forthcoming after a year of work and correspondence, Kennedy informed Veitch and Lucasfilm's director of publishing, Lucy Wilson, that he would have to leave *Dark Empire* and seek other work. This was a serious blow to the project, for the unique style of Kennedy's watercolor painted pages would be nearly impossible for any other artist to replicate. Wilson and Veitch both wrote to Kennedy in Scotland, begging him to stay on the project. But when the contract still didn't appear a few months later, Kennedy said he couldn't wait any longer, and Veitch recommended to Wilson other artists who could finish the series, among them Andy and Adam Kubert, who were just starting out in the business, but would later become legends in their own right.

VISIONS OF THE FUTURE

Potentially losing Kennedy as an artist wasn't the only difficulty Veitch had to deal with to keep the project afloat. Though Veitch had first approached Lucasfilm about creating a *Star Wars* comic back in November 1988, in the intervening year Bantam Books had acquired the license to publish *Star Wars* novels. At first, both sides were told not to worry. The comics and the novels could co-exist separately, as they had during their previous incarnations. But soon it became clear that Bantam's novels would be set in the same post-*Return of the Jedi* time period as was *Dark Empire*, and the events that happened in them might interfere with or contradict what Veitch had planned for his series. Fans would undoubtedly question what was the "official" story and what was not. Sales could be affected if one story was dismissed in favor of the other. Therefore, a continuity between the series needed to be established in a way never before realized for a licensed property.

"At the time we did *Dark Empire*, there wasn't as much weight paid to an integrated universe—we're talking early 1990s, before *The Phantom Menace* had come out—and some of the novels [*Splinter of the Mind's Eye*, ed.] had already been retconned out of existence. It was all being frantically created at the same time," says Barbara Kesel, who would later come aboard to edit *Dark Empire*. "I do remember a miniature freak-out in the office when we learned that twins were in the offing for Leia, when our story had focused more on the idea of [a] 'child.'"

Lucasfilm did not have a Keeper of the Holocron or Story Group at the time, so much of the handling of continuity fell into the laps of Tom Veitch and the author of the Bantam novels, Timothy Zahn. Like any two artists (or any two fans), they each had their own visions of what *Star Wars* was and consequently where to take the

Right, from top:
Dave Dorman's
stunning pencil work
for the cover of the
first issue; Boba Fett
(and Dengar!) makes
a surprise comeback.

Opposite page:
The terrifying World
Devastator makes
its presence felt
on Mon Calamari.

story and the characters. Zahn
had made his reputation on
military sci-fi novels, and took his
trilogy of novels in that direction,
writing page-turners that focused
on an Imperial admiral's ingenious
campaign to restore the Empire.
Veitch, too, respected the military
aspects of *Star Wars*, but his
background in philosophy and
theology (as a former Benedictine
monk) sparked his interest in its
mythological and moral roots. As
in all great stories, setting and
character are intricately linked—
and in the case of *Star Wars*, it
appeared to Veitch that George
Lucas had created his fictional
universe to explore an individual's
spiritual development. Since the
original *Star Wars* trilogy was
about Luke Skywalker embracing
his connection to the good (or
light) side of the "Force," thereby
redeeming his evil father, Veitch
perceived the next logical step
would be Luke's temptation by
the corrupting influence of
ultimate power. This echoes many
of the great myths and biblical
stories, where in order to fully
comprehend and join the light,
a hero must venture into the
deepest regions of the dark.

"The main inspiration comes
from C.G. Jung, who advises
'integrating the Shadow' as
necessary to personal growth.
Taking the 'heroic' position of
endlessly fighting the bad guys just
leads to stasis... and even defeat.
In my opinion, both Obi-Wan and
Yoda would have 'secret knowledge'
of the dark side," says Veitch.

As a veteran in comics,
Veitch understood he was writing
for a visual medium that relied
on fantastical illustrations and
scenarios for its storytelling power.
Consequently, he resolved to risk
excess when scripting his panels
and images, as the *Star Wars* films
had, rather than play it safe. He
backed up the big visual moment
in issue one—the Force Storm—by
explaining it was
not a chaotic
super weapon,
but a "function
of two powerful
minds focused
on each other:
Luke and the
Emperor. It's as
if a wormhole in
the Force had
opened between
them, causing a
massive release
of energy." In
creating the
darksiders
on Byss, he
referenced such
societies as the
Assassins' Guild
under Hassan-I
Sabbah, Hitler's

Gestapo, and even the dark angels
serving Satan. "The attempt to
create a stable society based on
the power of the dark side is what
the Emperor—and *Star Wars*—is all
about," Veitch wrote to Lucasfilm.

Most importantly, he argued
that Luke could learn about the
dark side without being devoured
by it. "The 'secrets' of the dark side
must be assimilated in order for the
dark side to be finally conquered.
Otherwise there is only endless
combat, endless war, numberless
deaths. Here we are working with
the principal that's described in
Jungian psychology as 'integration
of the Shadow.' See into your
Enemy and learn finally that he
has an aspect of *yourself*. This
simple idea is the key to what I'm
trying to do. It's there in the films,
and the relationship of Luke and
his father. Ultimately it must
be shown to be true in Luke's
relationship to the Emperor—
and to the dark side."

Veitch recognized a
simple solution to prevent any
contradictions that could arise
between his series and Zahn's:
Dark Empire could be set shortly
after Zahn's trilogy and he would
write an opening crawl to bridge

the two series. Lucasfilm agreed. This set a precedent for *Star Wars* continuity. Stories would be logged on a timeline, which would give direction for future artists and writers, but not inhibit their talents and unique perspectives. This kind of creative freedom was one of the reasons that the expanded *Star Wars* universe became so bold, interesting, and sometimes beautifully strange.

By late 1990, however, Veitch's solutions might all be in vain if *Dark Empire* could not find a sure path to publication.

A DARK HORSE TO THE RESCUE

While the editorial shift at Marvel put the project in limbo, a new party inquired with Lucasfilm regarding the *Star Wars* comic license. Dark Horse Comics owner Mike Richardson had seen some of Cam Kennedy's art for issue one. At the San Diego Comic Con

in 1990, he approached Lucy Wilson about acquiring *Dark Empire* for publication. Dark Horse had great success publishing comics based on other movie projects, such as *Aliens*, and felt they could do the same with *Star Wars*. Moreover, Dark Horse was willing to wait until Kennedy was finished with his other projects and negotiate properly for his services. "Mike Richardson told Lucy, 'Cam is just the best *Star Wars* artist in comics. Nobody else even comes close,'" Veitch wrote to Kennedy in December 1990.

Though Marvel lobbied to continue forward with the project, Lucasfilm decided to grant the *Star Wars* license to Dark Horse, beginning a 23-year chapter in *Star Wars* comics that ended only recently.

More importantly, *Dark Empire* had found a home.

CAM KENNEDY'S *STAR WARS*

The wait for Cam Kennedy to rejoin the project proved worth it. Though he had never watched the *Star Wars* films until he became involved in the project, he rendered the characters, the vehicles, and the worlds of the galaxy so confidently and so completely in his own style of painted watercolors that fans, critics, and other major artists noticed. Original *Star Wars* concept artist Ralph McQuarrie even wrote that he looked at Kennedy's art with "envy."

Kennedy himself warmly recalls an encounter with one of the industry's giants. "I remember speaking to Mœbius," says Kennedy, of the famous French artist, "when we both happened to be at a New York convention and I had some of my *Dark Empire* pages with me. He came over and said, 'Ahh, we must exchange pages.' And I said, 'Which ones would you like?' So he picked a page and then he went and got one of his pages and we swapped pages."

"THE IMAGES YOU ARE SEEING ARE BEING TRANSMITTED AT THIS VERY MOMENT FROM *CALAMARI*, ADMIRAL ACKBAR'S HOME PLANET--

"--THE MON CALAMARI HAVE BEEN A *PROUD* PART OF THE ALLIANCE SINCE THE *BEGINNING*-- IT'S NO WONDER THE ENEMY HAS CHOSEN TO TURN ON *THEM* WITH THESE PLANET SMASHERS... ISN'T THAT TRUE, ADMIRAL ACKBAR?"

"VERY TRUE... MANY YEARS AGO THE *MON CALAMARI* WERE CONSCRIPTED AS *SLAVE LABORERS* BY THE EMPEROR... WHEN WE RESISTED, OUR CITIES WERE ATTACKED, TO SET AN *EXAMPLE* FOR THE REST OF THE GALAXY--

"--BUT THIS EXPERIENCE ONLY HARDENED MY PEOPLE'S WILL TO *RESIST*-- AND TRANSFORMED THEM INTO FORMIDABLE FIGHTERS FOR THE ALLIANCE!

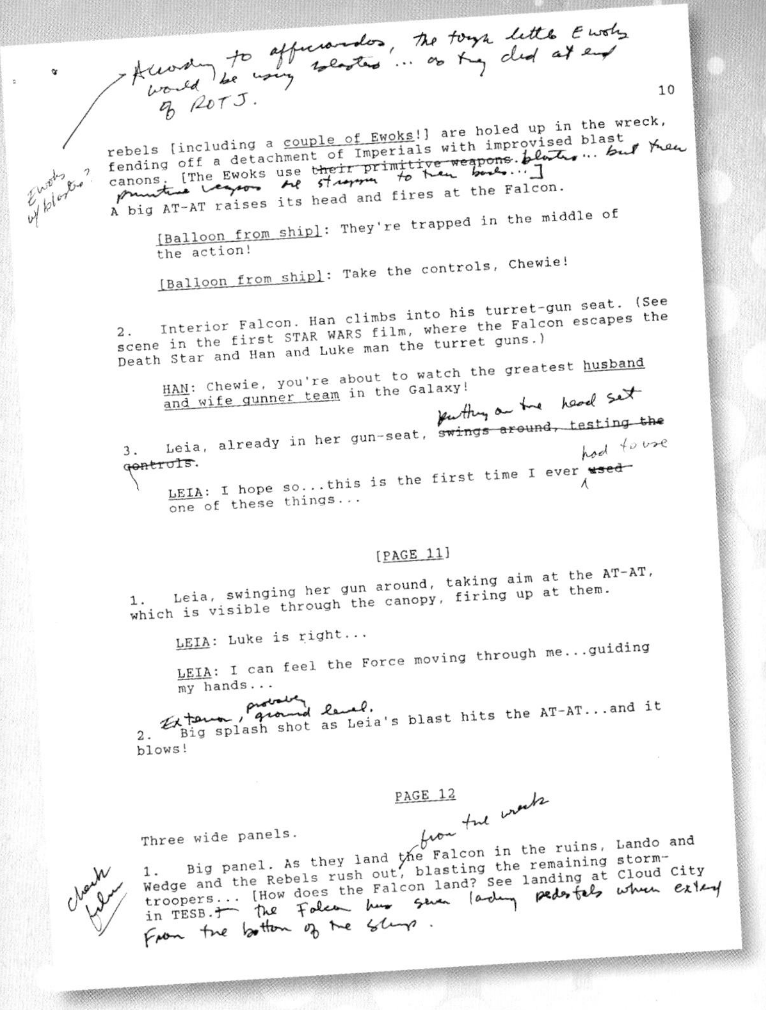

"At the time we approached Lucasfilm, it was generally understood that there would be no more *Star Wars* films, and the comics franchise was dead. Both Cam and I saw that as a golden opportunity. Then, when Lucas gave us 'carte blanche' to imagine the post-*Return of the Jedi Star Wars* universe, I leaped at the opportunity to explore the mythological underpinnings of the Force—both the light side and the dark side.

So, in the text pages for the very first *Dark Empire* comic, I wrote:

'A Jedi, from the beginning, must do what most men cannot: develop a sensitivity to the very existence of the Force. He must actually feel it, feel his oneness with it, feel it tangibly flowing through him, and then his conscious awareness must join the Force, so that the knowledge available through the Force becomes his own. At some point a Jedi learns to abandon reliance on his own mind and its effort. He learns to stretch out with his feelings, to let go of his limited idea of himself, and to move with the deeply instinctive levels of his being. By listening, by becoming peaceful, by turning his attention to the Force, he finds that place where his individuality is joined to the knowledge and power of the Universe.'

Opposed to this knowledge is the dark side, which channels the Force through anger, the will-to-power, unfettered violence, and instilling fear in the weak-minded. Luke's father followed that path to power—and to his own destruction. Thus, as the films made clear, Luke Skywalker has both sides of the Force in him. I am thinking especially of the scene in *The Empire Strikes Back* where Luke enters the cave on Dagobah and has a vision of Darth Vader—then, after decapitating Vader, discovers his own face behind Vader's mask!

Master Yoda showed Luke that shadow of himself so he would know that both the light side and the dark side of the Force were his (genetic) heritage. And Luke understood that in order to free himself—and his family—he had to penetrate that vision of himself and make it give up its secrets.

Thus it seemed to us (and to Archie Goodwin as well), there would inevitably arise the story of what happens when a Jedi Knight takes it upon himself to enter and investigate the dark mind of his father. Theoretically this could be an epic story exploring the deeper meaning of *Star Wars*—a character story beyond blasters, lightsaber duels, and explosive warship battles among the stars.

But Master Yoda warned him it would not be easy. His real strength would always be the light side of the Force: 'Remember, a Jedi's strength flows from the Force. But beware. Anger, fear, aggression. The dark side are they. Once you start down the dark path, forever will it dominate your destiny. Luke... Luke... do not... do not underestimate the powers of the Emperor, or suffer your father's fate you will.'"

The art of *Dark Empire* advertised for itself. One didn't need to be a fan of *Star Wars* or superhero comics to appreciate it. "Cam's painted art was a striking new approach for comics, let alone 'licensed' comics," says former Dark Horse editor, Barbara Kesel. "The intense colors and watercolor approach were so visually different from the average comics of the time that the series would have stood out on the stands even without a good story."

AN EMPIRE FOR THE AGES

When issue one of *Dark Empire* premiered in December 1991, three years after Veitch had sent his first letter to Lucasfilm, it stunned the comics world, selling hundreds of thousands of copies both in issues and as collected graphic novels. Filmmaker George Lucas, an avid comic book art collector himself, was so impressed

GEORGE LUCAS, AN AVID COMIC BOOK ART COLLECTOR HIMSELF, WAS SO IMPRESSED HE GAVE COPIES OF *DARK EMPIRE* TO HIS EMPLOYEES AS THE ANNUAL LUCASFILM CHRISTMAS GIFT.

[Script page, handwritten and typed:]

According to *afficionados*, the tough little Ewoks would be wiping *blasters* ... as they did at end of ROTJ.

10

Ewoks w/blasters?

rebels [including a couple of Ewoks!] are holed up in the wreck, fending off a detachment of Imperials with improvised blast canons. [The Ewoks use their primitive weapons *blasters* ... but their *primitive weapons are stronger to them books...*]

A big AT-AT raises its head and fires at the Falcon.

[Balloon from ship]: They're trapped in the middle of the action!

[Balloon from ship]: Take the controls, Chewie!

2. Interior Falcon. Han climbs into his turret-gun seat. (See scene in the first STAR WARS film, where the Falcon escapes the Death Star and Han and Luke man the turret guns.)

HAN: Chewie, you're about to watch the greatest husband and wife gunner team in the Galaxy!

3. Leia, already in her gun-seat, *putting on the head set* swings around, testing the controls.

LEIA: I hope so...this is the first time I ever *used* *had to use* one of these things...

[PAGE 11]

1. Leia, swinging her gun around, taking aim at the AT-AT, which is visible through the canopy, firing up at them.

LEIA: Luke is right...

LEIA: I can feel the Force moving through me...guiding my hands...

2. *Exterior, probably ground level.* Big splash shot as Leia's blast hits the AT-AT...and it blows!

PAGE 12

Three wide panels. *from the wreck*

Check film

1. Big panel. As they land the Falcon in the ruins, Lando and Wedge and the Rebels rush out, blasting the remaining storm-troopers... [How does the Falcon land? See landing at Cloud City in TESB.] *the Falcon has seen landing pedestals when exiting from the bottom of the ships.*

2

hyperspace. This would be a small clue, a <u>setup</u> for what <u>might</u> happen later in our story.

Roll-up:

Following the destruction of the second DEATH STAR, and the deaths of DARTH VADER and THE EMPEROR, an ominous calm descended over the Galaxy.

Then, Without warning, the worlds of the Imperial System erupted in civil war, as factions within the Imperial Navy battled the Emperor's ruling circle for control of the Empire.

In the meantime, The Rebel Alliance had regrouped its forces on the rim of the Galaxy. Broadcasting their cry of rebellion from an uncharted outpost world, the Rebels now launched wave after wave of warships into the conflict that raged at the Galactic Core.

The Rebel assaults were hit-and-run operations, designed to sow confusion among the feuding Imperials, and thus hasten the ultimate restoration of the Republic.

Long years of struggle passed, and for a time it seemed the Galaxy might descend into a state of perpetual anarchy...

* * *

This will be an interesting scene, as THE MILLENNIUM FALCON and TWO ALLIANCE ESCORT FRIGATES come out of hyperspace <u>amidst the wreckage and remains of a great space battle.</u> [For Escort Frigates, see <u>Sourcebook</u>, p 30-31.]

The Falcon and the Alliance ships are on a rescue mission: A captured Star Destroyer, manned by LANDO CALRISIAN and LUKE SKYWALKER, has crashed in the IMPERIAL CITY, on the ruling world of the great Imperial System.

The kind of splash layout we want to use here, for maximum visual effect, follows a style developed by Al Williamson: large visuals, possibly bleeds, will depict the large-scale action and special effects. Small inset panels or cut-outs will cut to interiors, showing the characters and most of the dialogue.

<u>Much of the book would consist of these kinds of layouts, giving Cam the maximum opportunity to paint "Star Wars-scale" visuals.</u> When these splash-layouts are used, the character panels would be always in the same positions, so that the reader has an expectation of where to look.

Here, for example, is a sketch of the kind of layout we would see on pages 2-3:

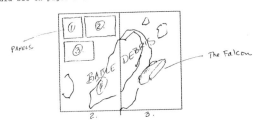

PANELS — BATTLE DEBRIS — The Falcon

PANEL 1.

HAN SOLO, at the controls of the MILLENNIUM FALCON, looking grim and a bit worried, staring straight at the reader. PRINCESS LEIA, standing behind him, also looking at the camera with a worried expression. Han would wear his traditional outfit. She's dressed for action -- most likely wearing a costume we haven't seen before.

As mentioned in the proposal, they are five or six years older, and they are now married!

Perhaps One of her hands is resting lightly on Han's shoulder.

(Note: there are two tall seats behind the pilot + co-pilot seats in the M.F. cockpit. Leia might be standing in two shot... the strapping herself in in scene 2.)

WITH ALL HIS HATRED FUNNELED INTO THE DEATH STORM, THE MALEVOLENT GENIUS IS CAUGHT OFF GUARD BY THE INVISIBLE WAVE OF *LIFE ENERGY* SURGING OVER HIM, SEPARATING HIM FROM HIS POWER--

ENVELOPED IN LIGHT, CUT OFF FROM HIS GREAT RAGE, THE EMPEROR FINDS HIMSELF UNABLE TO *CONTROL* THE DARK POWER HE HAS UNLEASHED--

--AND THE CATACLYSMIC *STORM* TURNS AGAINST ITS MAKER!

by it he gave copies of the graphic novel away to his employees as the annual Lucasfilm Christmas gift. Most of all, its incredible success changed how licensed properties were handled in the industry. In the past, publishers placed their lower grade talent on licensed comics because conventional wisdom held that the logo would sell a book over the art or story. *Dark Empire*, however, took the opposite approach, with Veitch and Kennedy treating it as highly as they would their original work. This made other top creators want to put their own indelible mark on properties like *Star Wars*.

"Tom loved the *Star Wars* stories and wanted to add a vision of his own to the mythos. He embraced the idea of the comic book as a novel and worked to make it epic," Kesel says. "Add in the Dave Dorman covers, and you had a comic that fans just couldn't ignore. It looked more 'grown-up' than the previous Marvel series and gave off a sense that you should take it seriously, and fans did. *Star Wars* fans were reaching their adult years, so they responded favorably to the series, and comics themselves were growing up and being taken more seriously. It was the right project at the right time, in addition to being just right."

Dark Empire remains perhaps the most spectacular *Star Wars* comic ever produced, and many would argue that few other comics since even come close. But to Veitch, it isn't so much a spectacle as it is, "a character story beyond blasters, lightsaber duels, and explosive warship battles among the stars." It is a story where even the greatest of galactic heroes, Luke Skywalker, must confront his dark side.

And even Luke Skywalker must be redeemed. ☮

MORE TO SAY

Dark Empire is available from Marvel.

The Light and Darkness War is out now.

Follow Michael Kogge online at www.michaelkogge.com or on twitter @michaelkogge.

HAVE YOU?

STAR WARS REBELS REVELATIONS!

STAR WARS

INSIDER

®

INSIDER REVEALS THE

50

"I WAS AN IMPERIAL OFFICER!"
Tales from the front line!

GREATEST REASONS TO LOVE THE *STAR WARS* PREQUELS!

JABBA'S RIGHT HAND MAN!
Bib Fortuna on life in the palace!

TITAN
ISSUE 147
FEB/MAR
2014

US $7.99
CAN $9.99

KEVIN J. ANDERSON
JEDI SCRIBE

ISSUE 147
FEB/MAR 2014

Star Wars: Honor Among Thieves by James S. A. Corey, published by Del Rey (March)

Issues 5 and 6 of *The Star Wars*, J.W.Rinzler's 8-part adaptation of George Lucas's 1974 rough draft screenplay, published by Dark Horse Comics

Star Wars: The Clone Wars: The Lost Missions released on Netflix (March)

A prolific author with his name on at least 50 *Star Wars* projects, Kevin J. Anderson is one of *Star Wars* Legends' most distinctive voices—and one of the rare few who span the disciplines of comic and prose writing. His *Star Wars* comic-book series *Tales of the Jedi* was a huge hit with fans, and his novels appealed to young and older readers alike.

This profile by Michael Kogge features some wonderful rarities, such as a list of Jedi Academy trilogy names considered for the first book, and a beautifully hand-written and illustrated letter sent to Anderson by *Star Wars* conceptual artist Ralph McQuarrie.—**Jonathan Wilkins**

Kevin James Anderson *(born March 27, 1962) has written spin-off novels for* Star Wars, StarCraft, Titan A.E., *and* The X-Files. *He is the co-author of the* Dune *prequel series and has written several comic books, including* Predator *and* The X-Files. *Anderson's superhero novels include* Enemies & Allies, *about the first meeting of Batman and Superman, and* The Last Days of Krypton, *telling the story of how Superman's planet Krypton came to be destroyed.*

AUTHORS OF THE EXPANDED UNIVERSE
KEVIN J. ANDERSON

OF ALL THE AUTHORS, ARTISTS, AND FILMMAKERS WHO HAVE TOLD STORIES IN THE *STAR WARS* EXPANDED UNIVERSE, NONE HAVE SPENT MORE TIME TRAVELING ITS HYPERLANES THAN KEVIN J. ANDERSON. HIS WORK SPANS THE ERAS, CHRONICLING BOTH THE ANCIENT JEDI KNIGHTS AND LUKE SKYWALKER'S LATER EFFORTS TO RE-BUILD THEIR ORDER. ANDERSON WAS THE FIRST *STAR WARS* WRITER TO ANTICIPATE A BEING'S GENETIC TIES TO THE FORCE, THE FIRST TO GIVE READERS A GLIMPSE OF THE EXPANDED UNIVERSE'S INCARNATION OF THE SPICE MINES OF KESSEL, AND ALSO THE FIRST TO HAVE A MOVIE CHARACTER DIE IN HIS NOVEL. WITH HIS NAME ON MORE THAN 50 *STAR WARS* PROJECTS, ANDERSON HAS PROBABLY INFLUENCED THE *STAR WARS* UNIVERSE MORE THAN ANY OTHER EXPANDED UNIVERSE AUTHOR.

WRITER AT BIRTH

Right (this page): Kevin J. Anderson's *Star Wars* Tales of the Jedi: *The Fall of the Sith Empire* #5

Right (opposite page, clockwise from top): Bestselling author Kevin J. Anderson; *Star Wars* Young Jedi Knights: *Trouble on Cloud City*; *Star Wars* Tales of the Jedi: *The Sith War*

Growing up in a small farming town in Wisconsin, Kevin James Anderson never struggled with the adolescent dilemma of figuring out what he wanted to be. He was born March 27, 1962, and by the moment he read his first science fiction tale, he knew he wanted to be a writer. By age eight, he commandeered his father's typewriter to bang out his own short stories. His initial attempt, "Injection," told of a mad scientist's serum that brought wax museum monsters to life. Over time, his stories became more complex as he read the titans of the genre, finding inspiration in the works of Frank Herbert, Andre Norton, and H.G. Wells. As a junior in high school, Anderson received his first printed byline when a Wisconsin student writing magazine published his post-apocalyptic story "Memorial." He studied physics, astronomy, and Russian history in college, continuing to write in his free time, unable to stop committing to paper the stories that wouldn't leave his imagination.

Just as Luke Skywalker seemed of a different breed than his aunt and uncle, Anderson's creativity stood out from his more pragmatic parents. His father served as a bank president and his mother worked as an accountant, and though they supported their son's literary endeavors, they also recognized the economic realities of the world. "They were very insistent on getting a 'real job,' [to] make sure you can make a living and pay the bills," says Anderson. "I didn't like it when I was a kid, because they were quashing my dreams. But it was a good thing for them to force me to be realistic."

STAR WARS
TALES OF THE JEDI
The Fall of the Sith Empire

DARK HORSE COMICS

FALL OF THE SITH EMPIRE
5 OF 5

$2.95 US
$4.10 CAN

DIRECT SALES

Anderson • Carrasco • Heike

DAYS AT THE LAB, NIGHTS IN THE STARS

After graduating from the University of Wisconsin, Anderson followed his parents' advice to get a "real job", with one caveat: He would make his living by writing, no matter the subject. He found employment as a technical writer at the Lawrence Livermore National Laboratory in northern California and worked there for 12 years, writing documentation about everything from respirators and lasers to top-secret government projects. When his day job ended, Anderson would go home, sit down at his keyboard, and proceed to write well into the night, turning his technical knowledge into fiction. He submitted stories and articles to magazines, placing a few while amassing a pile of rejection letters. Yet Anderson never gave up, and in 1988, at age 25, Signet Books bought the novel he had been working on for four years, *Resurrection, Inc.* "I got the phone call from my agent when I was in my office. That was one of those life-changing days," Anderson remembers. "Very promptly after that he sold a fantasy trilogy of mine [*Gamearth*]. So I went from having no books sold to having four books sold in a two or three-month period."

Anderson recognized having a couple of published novels under his belt didn't guarantee a writing career, so he continued his day job at Lawrence Livermore. There he found collaborators for future novels in scientist Doug Beason and his technical editor Rebecca Moesta, who would later become his wife. He and Beason were having success writing high-tech thrillers for Bantam-Spectra when Bantam announced that they had secured the *Star Wars* publishing license and selected Timothy Zahn to write a new trilogy set after the classic films. Anderson was so busy working at the lab and writing his own books that the news "wasn't really on my radar," he says.

THE *STAR WARS* BOOKS "WEREN'T REALLY ON MY RADAR."

KEYS TO THE GALAXY

Not soon after *Heir to the Empire* was published in 1991, Anderson received a surprise phone call from his Bantam editor. "Did he like *Star Wars*?" *Of course* he liked *Star Wars*! When it came out in his sophomore year of high school, he and his buddies saw it 15 times. Then would he be interested in writing three sequels? "It took me about a nanosecond to come up with the answer to that one," Anderson says.

The editor explained that Zahn's novels were just the beginning of an entirely new *Star Wars* fiction line. Bantam had recommended Anderson as a potential author to Lucasfilm Licensing because he wrote colorful, fast-paced adventures. The plan was that Anderson's new novels would follow Zahn's and that they would be published months apart in 1994, instead of the year-long publication gap between the books of Zahn's trilogy.

In 1992, armed with a printed hardback of *Heir to the Empire*, an advance review copy of *Dark Force Rising*, and Zahn's draft manuscript of *The Last Command* as his research materials, Anderson started outlining his trilogy. With six months to write each novel, he grew excited at the prospects of expanding a galaxy he'd loved since he was a teenager. Seeing *Star Wars* in the summer of 1977 had been a transformative experience for the young Anderson. "If you can think about never having seen anything like this before, sitting in the movie theater when the opening credits roll up... and then the Star Destroyer comes over your head, I mean that's like wet-your-pants, drop-your-jaw kind of stuff," remembers Anderson. "It's hard for maybe younger people, who have seen such big, spectacular stuff, to understand how earth-shaking that was. And we knew from the very moment we saw it that science fiction had changed forever."

My first page of random title suggestions for Book 1

```
JEDI DAWN
JEDI ACADEMY
JEDI STUDIES
JEDI SEARCH
JEDI QUEST
JEDI MASTER, JEDI APPRENTICE
THE JEDI PATH
SECRETS OF THE JEDI
JEDI SECRET
JEDI WISDOM
WISDOM OF THE JEDI
THE NEW ORDER OF JEDI KNIGHTS
```

The New Jedi Knights

```
     None of these really grab me at the moment, but perh
some combination will work.  These are just some rough
```

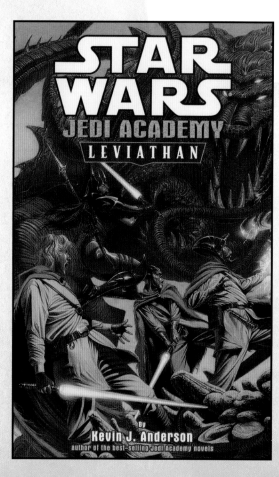

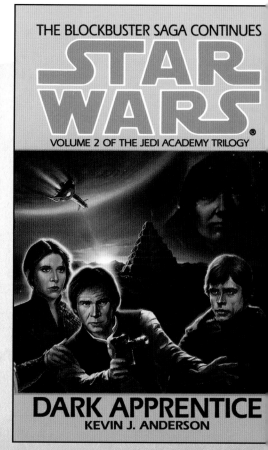

April 16, 1993

Dear Kevin,

Ahhhh -- just the kind of question I love to be asked.

Other ordinary English words for what Luke has: **Academy** comes from the name of a public garden near Athens where philosophers hung out and talked to anyone who'd listen. Another such garden was the **Lyceum**, and today that's also a word for a school. Still another bunch of philosophers hung out at the **Stoas** -- there were two or three of them, a kind of shopping mall open on one side, in the middle of town. This was where the "Stoic" philosophy got its name. Jedi Lyceum, Jedi Stoa . . . I dunno. And I don't at all like Jedi **Seminary**, even though one of the novelizations refers to Luke wearing a cassock. **Campus, cloister, quad** (that's the square of grass inside a cloister at Oxford or Cambridge) -- I doubt it.

The Force is pretty clearly the Taoist **Ch'i**, though the usual translation of that word is "breath, spirit." The use of ch'i was taught in the Shaolin **Temple** or **Monastery**. I don't think you want either of those. In Japanese, ch'i is **ki** and its use is taught in a **dojo**. (The element **do** derives from the Chinese **tao**, "way," meaning both path and method, just as it does in English.) Jedi Dojo has an ugly grating sound to it. Also, dojo is perhaps not a word recognized easily in Europe. When we were over for the 1990 worldcon, I noticed advertising for Teenage Mutant Hero Turtles -- the full phrase in English, not the local language, so I can't remember what country it was in.

Cadre is French, so I checked it in a French dictionary to see if there might be a usable related term. No luck; there was simply a stern notation that grammarians dislike the word in its current use for a trained person in authority. Cadre meaning a skeleton group of officers is a special use of a word meaning a picture-frame or a framework of any kind. No help there.

So we go to the classical languages. Force as a noun is **vis** in Latin, **bia** in Greek. As a verb, the stem is **cog-** in Latin, **dyn-** in Greek. To work is **labor-** or **erg-** respectively. **Laboratory**? Wrong connotations. Working with the Force: **Dynurgy**. (Trust me, the vowel does change to u. Think of **metallurgy** and **demiurge**.) Still, Dynurgy doesn't sound like an institution of learning, rather something that's learned there.

A Jedi Knight has his religio-mystical side, but he is not contemplative. If he practices any kind of meditation, it is something like the Zen swordsman's meditation of awareness of his surroundings. He does not think -- "Trust the Force, Luke " -- he acts. The Greek word for action is **praxis**, and the word is used in English to refer to the actual doing of something, as opposed to theory. **Practice** and **pragmatic** come from it. Again, praxis sounds more like what is learned, not the place of learning. Tacking on the common Greek ending for a place belonging to this-or-that, we get **Praxeion**; the more familiar Latinized version gives **Praxeum**. Jedi Praxeum? Well, Luke is going to have to explain what the place is all about, so he might as well define it: "a place for the learning of action." Or however you want to phrase it. I enclose dictionary photocopies, with notations.

If this doesn't help, ask again!

Best, Karen

JEDI QUESTS, ANGRY ADMIRALS

In the late 1980s, Brian Daley, author of the *Han Solo Adventures*, proposed a *Star Wars* series to Del Rey that took a more mythological approach to the universe than the militaristic one Zahn would later write. Daley believed the adventures of Luke Skywalker after *Return of the Jedi* should have him focused on seeking out potential Jedi Knights as if he was King Arthur forming the Knights of the Round Table. Unaware of Daley's proposal, Anderson gave Luke a similar goal. In the three novels (*Jedi Search*, *Dark Apprentice*, and *Champions of the Force*) that became The Jedi Academy Trilogy, Luke's quest was to find beings sensitive to the Force so as to rebuild the Jedi Order. In doing so, Anderson anticipated the genetic connection to the Force that George Lucas would reveal in *The Phantom Menace*. Anderson created a Jedi-reader device that allowed Luke to detect and measure a being's strength in the Force. "It was a way that we could begin our Jedi search. Because otherwise, what do you do, go door-to-door and just try to touch somebody and see if you sense the Force in this one?" says Anderson. "[Or] have people bend spoons in front of you?"

Anderson also followed the military angle of Zahn's books, inventing an isolated Imperial weapons laboratory that was inspired directly from Anderson's experience at Lawrence Livermore. Like the pulp stories of old about Japanese soldiers marooned on remote islands, and then rescued years after World War II ended, Anderson envisioned these Imperials had been cut off from contact with the rest of the galaxy, and only when they emerged years later did they realize the Rebel Alliance had won.

To lead the facility, Anderson created Admiral Daala, a fiery commander who could challenge the fledgling New Republic yet was a marked contrast to Zahn's brilliant strategist, Grand Admiral Thrawn. "I wanted somebody who was a little more of a loose cannon," Anderson says. "I thought she was edgy, and dangerous, and a little bit unpredictable. And not the completely cool and analytical tactical genius."

He planned to kill her off in the second novel, *Dark Apprentice*, when his test readers revolted and threatened to "lock him in a closet like Kathy Bates from *Misery* until I wrote her back into the story," he says. He listened to them and then went on to feature her in a follow-up *Star Wars* novel, *Darksaber*. Almost 15 years after her last appearance in *Darksaber*, other authors would bring Daala back in the Legacy of the Force series, propelling her to new heights of villainy. "It's kind of a good thing that I did keep her alive, since she's now leading the Galactic Alliance," Anderson says, with a laugh.

CONNECTIONS OF THE FORCE

While writing The Jedi Academy Trilogy, a fan asked Anderson whether or not he was going to incorporate the elements of the Tom Veitch-Cam Kennedy comic, *Dark Empire*. Anderson hadn't heard of the Dark Horse series. Lucasfilm sent him the comics, but said he didn't have to take the story into account if he didn't want to. "I read them and I find out that Leia has another baby, the Emperor comes back, Luke goes to the dark side, and I thought this isn't really the sort of stuff you would forget the day afterward," he says.

Anderson contacted *Dark Empire*'s writer, Tom Veitch, and discovered Veitch was launching a prequel comic series about the Old Republic called *Tales of the Jedi*. The two men became good friends, and Anderson found a way to integrate more than just *Dark Empire* in his novels. Veitch invited Anderson to help script the second *Tales* series, *Dark Lords of the Sith*, and Anderson synergized his books with *Tales* by making Exar Kun, Luke's Sith antagonist in The Jedi Academy Trilogy, a central character in *Dark Lords*. Anderson would then take the reins from Veitch and script the rest of the *Tales of the Jedi* comics, going back in time in *The Golden Age of the Sith* and concluding the saga with *Redemption*.

Clockwise from above right: A Ralph McQuarrie sketch for *Star Wars: The Illustrated Universe*. Personal correspondance from McQuarrie to Anderson; *Star Wars: Young Jedi Knights: Heirs of the Force*, *Star Wars: Young Jedi Knights: Diversity Alliance*.

THE BESTSELLING SAGA CONTINUES!

STAR WARS
YOUNG JEDI KNIGHTS
DIVERSITY ALLIANCE

KEVIN J. ANDERSON
and REBECCA MOESTA
NEW YORK TIMES BESTSELLING AUTHORS OF SHARDS OF ALDERAAN

THE TWIN CHILDREN OF HAN AND LEIA EMBARK ON ALL-NEW STAR WARS ADVENTURES!

STAR WARS
YOUNG JEDI KNIGHTS
HEIRS OF THE FORCE

KEVIN J. ANDERSON
author of The Jedi Academy Trilogy
and REBECCA MOESTA

· ETERNAL FLAMS OF FAITH ·

THE GLEAMING,
BRIGHT, HIGHLY ESTEEMED
MEDAL OF TOLERANCE AWARDED
KEVIN J. ANDERSON
BY
R. McQ.

· ¢ ·

BECAUSE HE IS FEELING BAD ABOUT
NOT AKNOWLEGING BOOKS RECIVED.
INVITATIONS SEEMINGLY IGNORED ETC..
..···
LOOK FORWARD TO SEEING NEW
WORK ON THE STAR WARS UNIVERSE.

a

I'M STILL FINISHING UP SOME WORK
ON THE 'FORBIDEN PLANET' REMAKE
AND OTHER NONSENSE.

a

R.

SUN-CRUSHING CAREER

Accounting for all the *Star Wars* projects Anderson has done would require a Holocron of its own. He's very proud of the fourteen books in the Young Jedi Knights series he wrote with his wife, Rebecca Moesta, and also his shepherding of the *Star Wars Tales* short story series, which remain among the bestselling *Star Wars* anthologies of all time. But one project close to Anderson's heart is *The Illustrated Star Wars Universe*, on which he partnered with *Star Wars*'s original conceptual artist Ralph McQuarrie. For that book, Lucasfilm commissioned Anderson to develop the background of the worlds seen in new McQuarrie paintings. "That artbook was a special project for George, and he wanted it to be done right," Anderson says. McQuarrie was

about to retire and "he wanted this to be his last hurrah... to show off all of his work."

Since his time in *Star Wars*, Anderson's writing career has gone supernova. He writes eight to ten hours a day, seven days a week, publishing eight novels a year. He's expanded another famous sci-fi universe, that of *Dune*, in a series written with Frank Herbert's son, and has penned an original space opera he deems his masterpiece, *The Saga of Seven Suns*. As for returning to a galaxy of far, far away, Anderson admits he finds learning the new lore intimidating, with over 140 *Star Wars* books on the shelves. But he believes the sequel movies will open new avenues for the *Star Wars* Expanded Universe. "I'm a fan, still, at the core, and I'm pleased to hear that there will be more movies made, which are going to inspire all kinds of new creative work. And I will be there watching it."

SELECT BIBLIOGRAPHY

The Jedi Academy Trilogy (*Jedi Search, Dark Apprentice, Champions of the Force*; Bantam, 1994)

Darksaber (Bantam, 1994)

Tales of the Jedi comics (*Golden Age of the Sith, Fall of the Sith Empire, Dark Lords of the Sith, The Sith War, Redemption*; Dark Horse Comics, 1995-1998)

The Illustrated Star Wars Universe with Ralph McQuarrie (Bantam, 1995)

Tales from the Mos Eisley Cantina, Tales of the Bounty Hunters, Tales from Jabba's Palace (Bantam, 1995-1995)

Dune prequels and sequels, with Brian Herbert (Spectra and Tor, 1999-now)

The Young Jedi Knights series, with Rebecca Moesta (Berkeley, 1995-1998)

The Saga of Seven Suns series (Orbit, 2002-2008)

Dan Shamble, Zombie P.I. series (Kensington, 2011-now) *Clockwork Angels* with Neil Peart of *RUSH* (ECW Press, 2012)

Connect with Kevin J. Anderson on Twitter @TheKJA or www.wordfire.com.

"I'M A FAN, STILL, AT THE CORE."

┌─ **EXPANDED** ─

Follow Michael Kogge on twitter @michaelkogge.

└─ **UNIVERSE** ─┘

COMPLETE YOUR STAR WARS COLLECTION!

Rogue One: A Star Wars Story
The Official Collector's Edition
ISBN 9781785861574

Rogue One: A Star Wars Story
The Official Mission Debrief
ISBN 9781785861581

THE BEST OF STAR WARS INSIDER

The Best of Star Wars Insider
Volume One
ISBN 9781785851162

The Best of Star Wars Insider
Volume Two
ISBN 9781785851179

The Best of Star Wars Insider
Volume Three
ISBN 9781785851896

The Best of Star Wars Insider
Volume Four
ISBN 9781785851902

Lords of the Sith
ISBN 9781785851919

FOR MORE INFORMATION, VISIT: TITAN-COMICS.COM